GODSEED

GODSEED

THE JOURNEY OF CHRIST

JEAN HOUSTON

*This publication made possible with
the assistance of the Kern Foundation*

The Theosophical Publishing House

Wheaton, Ill. U.S.A.
Madras, India/London, England

The Theosophical Publishing House
P. O. Box 270
Wheaton, IL 60189-0270

A publication of the Theosophical Publishing House,
a department of the Theosophical Society in America

Library of Congress Cataloging-in-Publication Data

Houston, Jean.
    Godseed : the journey of Christ / by Jean Houston.
       p. cm.
    Originally published: Amity, N.Y. : Amity Press. 1988, in
series: Mythos books.
    "This publication made possible with the assistance of the
Kern Foundation."
    ISBN 0-8356-0677-5 : $11.95
    1. Jesus Christ—Miscellanea.   I. Title.
[BT304.93.H68   1992]
291.4'48—dc20   91-50761
                                            CIP

Printed in the United States of America
by Versa Press

**100% Recycled
Paper**

Contents

Preface

Anyone who writes a book about Jesus generally has some difficult personal issues with this leading archetype of the Western world, and I am no exception to this ancient rule. My issues have taken me on a long journey looking for the historical Jesus as well as the perennial Christ; for the Perfected One, as well as for the one who is deeply human; for the God-in-Man who is utterly other, and for the Man-In-God who is the Beloved of the soul. I have felt, as have so many others, rising nausea at the horrors and holocaust done in the name of Christ, and I have bowed in reverence before a simple act of Christian charity. I have struggled with the prism of theologies reflecting so many different ways of perceiving Jesus, and have known deep anguish at the polarizing effects these have had, dividing nation from nation, family from family, and setting up all kinds of ambivalence in the human soul. I myself, over the last year and a half, have received both acrimony and threats from fundamentalists for the kinds of views expressed in these pages. But I've also seen acts of unconditional loving kindness, and human service taken to its utmost from people who hold views of the Bible that permit only the most literal interpretation.

My journey has taken me through the widest spectrum of scholarly studies, including stints of teaching college courses in both Old and New Testament. My inspiration has been both orthodox and heterodox. I am inspired by the gnostic gospels as much as I am by the standard canon, by esoteric thinkers as well as by the great line of Christian thinkers from Origen and Saint Augustine to Karl Rahner, Hans Kung and Paul Tillich. But my early religious life was colored by my comedy-writer father who was, to say the least, irreverent. Nevertheless, he was the trigger for my first deeply religious experience.

It all began because my mother was a Sicilian Catholic with leanings toward Christian Science while my father was an Ambulatory Protestant. He had been born a Southern Baptist, but after falling in love with ladies of various Protestant sects and joining their churches he fell in love with my mother, a first-generation Sicilian born in Syracusa, with the name of Maria Graziella Seraphina Annuciata Fiorina Todaro. He had to become a Catholic in order to marry her. A young priest at St. Patrick's Cathedral gave him religious instruction. After six weeks of trading jokes instead of theology, the priest finally said, "Jack, you're just a natural-born pagan! Here, I'll gave you a kind of learner's permit so you can go ahead and get married. But any kids you and your wife have, you've got to promise to send them to Catholic school. We don't want them ending up like you!"

From that time on my father made an inseparable connection between comedy and religion. Religion was where the jokes were. Religion was where the girls were. Religion was the source of all piquant and funny things. When, at about the age of four, I asked my father to tell me about "sweet Jesus, meek and mild," I was answered with a hilarious description of Christ the Comedian. This view of Jesus was evenly tempered by my mother's portrayal of him as the Great Friend, the one who would be available for "deep talk" at all times and under any conditions.

When I turned five my father, who had up to that time been a writer on the Bob Hope show, got suspended from that show for a year due to "an excess of high spirits." We found ourselves broke and moving from California to live with my mother's parents for a year in the Sicilian section of Brooklyn, or "Brookalina" as my grandmother called it. My grandmother, Vita Todaro, I discovered, had her own church going on in the basement of her home for the older ladies of the community. Meeting every Sunday morning before the 11 a.m. mass, she would preach in Italian to her friends on spiritual subjects often having to do with the feminine aspect of God. There was, I recall, a great deal of devotion to the Madonna. When I asked one old lady in my grandmother's congregation why they didn't talk more about Jesus Christ, she answered with words not unlike those I heard from another old lady in Italy years later, "Because everybody knows it is the Mamma who does all of the work!" Then too, my grandmother put great emphasis on ways to enter into communion with the Holy Spirit. One must experience the Divine Life, she insisted, not just worship or talk about it. It was clear that the women found my grandmother's sermons and spiritual counseling much more interesting and relevant than those of the priest of the local Catholic Church we would all attend after my grandmother's services.

Though I have found beauty and inspiration in Catholicism since, the first time I went to the local church I was profoundly shocked. I had never been in a Catholic church before. The priest's sermon was filled with images of Jesus bringing hellfire and damnation to all who sinned against him, which, he made very clear, was everybody in the congregation. "Nana" I whispered to my grandmother, "is that my Jesus he's talking about?" "No, figlia mia," she whispered back. "Thatsa justa Jesu of the priests, not Jesu of you and me. You and me, we know the real Jesu."

After the service, I went up to the statue of Jesus at the front of the church. It was a particularly agonized crucified Christ imported from Sicily, very bloody and twisted with pain, and with a greenish cast to the body. This vision, coupled with the heavy smell of incense, and the priest's recent sermon made me feel sick to my stomach as well as in my soul. Something in me rebelled at that moment. I felt that the Jesus given to us by this church was not necessarily the one that God intended us to have. Things got even more complicated a few weeks later when my father remembered his promise to the priest who had given him religious instruction and sent me into the first grade at the local Catholic school. It didn't help that Dad would gag up my catechism and give me provocative questions to ask the nuns.

"Sister Theresa, when Ezekiel saw the wheel, do you suppose he was drunk?"

"Sister Theresa, I counted my ribs and I counted Joey Mangibella's ribs, and we have the same number of ribs. So if God took a rib out of Adam to make Eve like you said, how come . . . ?

Then there were all of the Jesus questions.

"Sister Theresa, how do you *know* that Jesus wasn't walking on the rocks below the surface when he seemed to be walking on the water?"

"Sister Theresa, when Jesus rose, was that because God filled him full of helium?"

You might think, perhaps, that the shy quaver of

a small child's voice framed these questions after school to the little nun when she and I were alone in the hush of an empty classroom. Not at all. They were presented with all the delicacy of a circus calliope in the middle of a class, and generally when the Mother Superior was visiting. Poor sweet Sister Theresa. Convent life had not prepared her for the theological thrusts of my comedy-writer father's imagination. He had by that time written for Amos and Andy, Fibber McGee and Molly, Fred Allen, Bob Hope, and Abbott and Costello, and with these eminent credentials he was ready to raise the comic consciousness of the Catholic Church.

"Blashphemy!" the good sister shouted one day after I asked her my very own question, the one that haunts the mind of almost every little Catholic child. I had checked out the question with Joey Mangiabella and Cookie Colozzi, and they assured me that they had been wondering about it too. I asked the question the day that the Mother Superior was visiting as I thought that she would be able to answer it if Sister Theresa couldn't.

I raised my hand. "Sister Theresa!"

"Yesh," she lisped, with a worried look at Mother Superior.

"Did Jesus ever have to go to the bathroom?.

"Blashphemy, Blashphemy, Blashphemy!" she lisped and raged as the good Mother Superior took a hurried exit. "Sacrilish and blashphemy!" And with the zeal of one possessed she stormed over to the supply closet, took out a large sheet of oak tag and a bottle of India ink, marched over to the bulletin board, tacked up the oak tag, and, in large black letters wrote:

JEAN HOUSTON'S YEARS IN PURGATORY

From that day on, any time I asked a question she thought I shouldn't have, especially about Jesus, Sister Theresa took out the bottle of India ink, climbed up on a stool, and X-ed up more years in purgatory, informing me at the same time that this was the will of Jesus. Each X stood for a hundred thousand years! By the end of the first grade, when I turned six, I had three hundred million years in purgatory to my credit.

On the day of the great addition, when the X's were totaled up, I returned home crushed by the vision of spending eternity being barbecued on a spit with time off to be on the swallowing end of millions of miles of Italian spaghetti. (There was something about Sister Theresa's theology that led her to equate endless torment with eating. Perhaps that's why she weighed only ninety-five pounds.)

With *major crisis* plastered all over my face, I stumbled into the house and refused to look at my father.

"What's the matter, kiddo?" he asked, eyeing me from his typewriter.

"Daddy," I blurted out, "I'm going to Purgatory for three hundred million years, and it's all your fault!"

"Greeeeat, Jeanie-pot-pie! You topped my lines! Keep that up and I'll put you on the air opposite Henny Youngman!"

"But it's true, Daddy! Sister Theresa added up all the years and says that because of the questions I ask in school I've got to go to purgatory for . . . why are you laughing? Stop laughing, Daddy! It's not funny!"

My father stopped howling long enough to swoop me up on his shoulders and start moving his feet to the sound of a train clicking along on the tracks.

"Watch out!" he hooted. "Here comes the Pur-

gatory Special! Purgatorypurgatorypurgatorypurga-
torypurgatory. Toot, toot!"

And gathering up steam, he raced with me out
the door and down the block, keeping up his "pur-
gatorypurgatorypurgatory" all the way.

High on his shoulders, I watched the amazed
faces of the Sicilian neighbors as we sped by. Occasionally one would scream from a window, "Eh, dere
goesa Crazy Jack! Eh, Crazy Jack, you betta watcha
outa or yousa gonna fall ana breaka da bambina's
head!"

As he leaped across the street, dodging motorists
but never losing the beat, I shouted, "Where are we
going, Daddy?"

"To the movies, honey-pot! To see how the real
saints had it. You think you got troubles? Wait'll you
see how they hogtied poor old Bernadette!"

Within minutes we were seated inside the
Brooklyn Fortway theater watching *The Song of Bernadette*, a 1940s classic starring Jennifer Jones as the
French peasant girl who saw a vision of Mary while
praying at the grotto in Lourdes. We were surrounded in the darkness by good Italian Catholics,
most of whom were watching this picture with the
reverence accorded the Pope. When Jennifer Jones
made her first appearance, the old lady sitting next to
me murmured *"Cue bella questa santa"* (what a beautiful saint) and crossed herself.

I was spellbound, and identified with Miss Jones
at every turn. When the spectral white vision of the
Virgin Mary appeared to Bernadette I had to resist an
urge to fall to my knees. Instead, I limited myself to a
verbal outpouring of religious devotion: "Oh boy! Oh
boy! Oh boy!"

The audience was entranced, the old lady beside
me was muttering, *"Ah Santa Vergine"* over and over

again, when suddenly—a long, loud, whinnying laugh exploded our reveries.

"Hyah . . . hyah . . . hyah . . .hee hee hee ha ha *ha ha hyah* . . . hyah . . . hyah . . . hee hee hee ha ha ha ha . . .!"

Beside me, my father, the source of this eruption, was striving mightily and unsuccessfully to contain himself.

"Daddy! Shhh! This is the holy part!"

"Yeah. I know," my father brayed. "But that's old Linda playing Mary! You remember Linda, honey? Linda Darnell? We met her at that party in Beverly Hills. Good old Linda. I told her she'd go far!"

And with that he sputtered and choked like an old Model T, only to dissolve helplessly into an unrelenting roar.

"Daddy," I ordered, desperate now. "Go to the bathroom!"

He obeyed, stepping over the knees of the old lady who stabbed the air in an evil gesture after him and hissed, "*Diablo . . . diablo!*"

He returned sometime later, semi-chastened, with only an occasional snort to remind us of his true feelings.

After the movie let out I began running home, heady with purpose. As I darted ahead of my father, he called out, "Hey Jeanie-pot, slow down. What's the matter? Are you mad at me? C'mon, take my hand—at least to cross the street. Where are you going, anyway?"

"I'm going to see the Virgin Mary," I replied, jerking my hand loose.

"Oh? Okay. Let's go together."

With that, he grabbed my hand again and began skipping and singing down the street, trying to lure me into a Dorothy and the Tin Man routine: "We're off to see the Virgin, the Wonderful Virgin of Lourdes. We'll join the hordes and hordes and hordes and hooooooordes . . . The hordes to see the Virgin of Lourdes. Wonderful Virgin of Lourdes. We're off . . ."

"Quit that, Daddy! I've got something to do. Let me go."

With a fierce tug, I broke free and raced down the street, only to call back, "And don't follow me! This is serious!"

Back at the house I loped up the stairs to one of the bedrooms that contained a large deep closet with a wall safe in the back of it. The clothes had been removed from this closet since Chickie had recently chosen to have her eight pups there and had continued to lease the area as a dog nursery.

"No doubt about it," I thought as I squinted speculatively into the closet. "It could easily pass for a grotto."

I scooped up the puppies and dragged a protesting Chickie out of her nesting spot. The "grotto" cleared, I bounced down on my knees, clapped my hands together in prayer, and, with an eye fixed on the dial of the wall safe prayed, "Please Virgin Mary, please pop up in the closet the way you did for Bernadette. I'd really like to see you. If you come I'll give up candy for a month . . . two months. Okay?"

No Virgin Mary.

"Uh, Virgin Mary? Listen. I'm going to shut my eyes and count to ten and you be there in the closet when I finish counting. Okay? 1-2-3-4-5-6-7-8-9-10."

No Virgin Mary—only the dog carrying one of her pups back by the scruff of the neck to the site of my hoped-for Visitation. I indignantly pulled them out again and kneeled down for serious business.

"Look, Virgin Mary? This time I'm going to count to . . . twenty-three, and when I open my eyes you try to come down from heaven and get into the closet. And I'll give up candy and cake and ice cream and chicken with garlic and lemon sauce. Okay?"

Well, she must have gotten lost, for she never did show up. At least not in the closet. I kept on trying for a while, counting to even higher numbers such as 52 . . . 87 . . . 103 . . . 167 . . . but all I ever opened my eyes to was an ever-growing melange of puppies. By this time I had given up all sugars, all starches and virtually all calories. The only thing I kept was broccoli, which I detested. Finally, I resigned myself to the fact that my efforts to lure heaven had failed. I gave up the ghost to the dogs, as it were.

Spent and unthinking, I sat down by the windowsill and looked out at the fig tree in the backyard. Sitting there drowsy and unfocused, I must in my innocence have done something right, for suddenly the key turned and the door to the universe opened. I didn't see or hear anything unusual. There were no visions, no bursts of light. The world remained the same. And yet everything around me, including myself, moved into meaning. Everything–the fig tree in the yard, the dogs in the closet, the wall safe, the airplane in the sky, the sky itself, and even my idea of the Virgin Mary–became part of a single Unity, a glorious symphonic resonance in which every part of the universe was a part of and illuminated every other part, and I knew that in some way it all worked together and was very, very good.

My mind dropped all shutters. I was no longer just the little local "I", Jean Houston, age six, sitting on a windowsill in Brooklyn in the 1940s. I had awakened to a consciousness that spanned centuries and was on intimate terms with the universe. I couldn't express it, but I knew that everything mattered. Nothing was alien or irrelevant or distant. The farthest star was right next door and the deepest mystery was clearly seen. It seemed to me as if I knew everything, as if I *was* everything. Everything–the fig tree, the pups in the closet, the planets, Joey Mangiabella's ribs, the mind of God, Linda Darnell, the chipped paint on the ceiling, the Virgin Mary, my Mary Jane shoes, galaxies, pencil stubs, the Amazon rain forest, my Dick and Jane reader, and all the music that ever was–was in a state of resonance and of the most immense and ecstatic kinship. I was in a universe of friendship and fellow feeling, a companionable universe filled with interwoven Presence and the Dance of Life.

Somewhere downstairs my father laughed and instantly the whole universe joined in. Great roars of hilarity sounded from sun to sun. Field mice tittered and so did the gods and so did the rainbows. Laughter leavened every atom and every star until I saw a universe spiraled by joy, not unlike the one described by Dante in his great vision in the Paradiso . . . *d'el riso del universo* (the joy that spins the universe).

Childhood kept these memories fresh. Adolescence electrified them and gave them passion, while first maturity dulled and even occasionally lost them. But even so, my life, both personal and professional, has been imbued ever since with the search for the unshuttered mind, the evocation and application of this mind in daily life and experience, and the conviction that human beings have within them the birthright of capacities for knowing and participating in a much larger and deeper Reality. From this springs a search for the cosmic connection, a living sense of the nature of reality, a theology of the Way Things Work. (1)

And what happened to my notions of Jesus in the midst of all this? After all, my childhood attempts to know him had laid the groundwork for what was to be my professional life in exploring and developing human capacities and cultural growth. The irony is that as I pursued my studies of the world's spiritual and psychological traditions, Jesus grew in mystery for me, but one that included equal portions of ambivalence as well as fascination. One could never forget the wars fought and the countless people persecuted over their interpretation as to who and what Jesus really was. On my travels all over the world I had seen too many instances of Christian missionary work gone sour. Too often I had seen native people who had once had a rich and fertile spiritual and mythic tradition, often thousands of years old, having these life-giving traditions demythologized, ridiculed and virtually destroyed by well-meaning clerics. And what were they given in its stead but an angry God whose religion was not one of love nor of honoring the healing and helping traditions of the native locale, but rather one of guilt and repentance and the methods and madness of the Western world. This is surely not what Jesus would have wanted. Yet for every terrible example of this, there are other instances of missionaries who honor the spiritual and native traditions of local peoples while preaching the *kerygma* of Christ. Still there is that merciless urge to convert that haunts Christianity as it does no other religion. Why must everyone accept human-Divine Love on the same terms? Maybe Jesus's message of the human-Divine connection and the primacy of Love was too much. Maybe the human race, as has often been observed, can take only a little reality.

To someone studying the infinite varieties of Christian theology it sometimes seems that there are as many Christs as there are Christians. He has been regarded as an ethical idealist and as the Creative Word of God; as a mystical contemplative and a social revolutionary; as the victim of a Jewish political tragedy and as the Man for all seasons and all places; as a completely made up mythological figure and as the very palpable center of history; as the lure of becoming and as the One who Was and Is and Ever Shall Be.

However or whoever Jesus may be, he continues to speak to the broadest and the deepest issues of the human condition. I write this book to pursue my own continuing search for Jesus. My search covers the orthodox, the gnostic, the esoteric, views of radical and traditional thinkers. Most of all, however, I am moved to write by the need to help others find inspiration great enough to deal with this most interesting and potent time in human history. As I wrote in the concluding pages of *The Possible Human:*

Never before has the responsibility of the human being for the planetary process been greater. Never before have we gained power of such magnitude over the primordial issues of life and death. The density and intimacy of the global village, along with the staggering consequences of our new knowledge and technologies, make us directors of a world that, up to now, has mostly directed us. This is a responsibility for which we have been ill prepared and for which the usual formulas and stop-gap solutions will not work.

We find ourselves in a time in which extremely limited consciousness has the powers once accorded to the gods. Extremely limited consciousness can launch a nuclear holocaust with the single push of a button. Extremely limited consciousness can and does intervene directly in the genetic code, interferes with the complex patterns of life in the sea, and pours its wastes into the protective ozone layers that encircle the earth. Extremely limited consciousness is about to create a whole new energy base linking together computers, electronics, new materials from outer space, biofacture, and genetic engineering, which in turn will release a flood of innovation and external power unlike anything seen before in human history. In short, extremely limited consciousness is accruing to itself the powers of Second Genesis. And this with an ethic that is more Faustian than godlike.(2)

Clearly, we have come into a *kairos*, a loaded time when we must humbly but tenaciously re-educate ourselves for sacred stewardship, acquiring the inner capacities to match our outer powers. We must seek and find those physical, mental, and spiritual resources that will enable us to partner the planet. I offer this experiential approach to the story of Jesus as one way in which to discover some of the resources necessary to a time and history when we are being called upon to live mythic lives, lives in which we must rise to become Christic if we would meet the challenges of our time.

I am grateful that Quest Books has decided to re-issue this book, and would caution the reader that however and wherever you look for the Christ, look first within your own heart.

NOTES

1. A somewhat different version of this story occurs in my book, *The Possible Human*. (Los Angeles: J. P. Tarcher, Inc., 1982), pp. 182-187.
2. Ibid, p. 213.

Acknowledgments

It is with pleasure and profound gratitude that I acknowledge those friends and associates who have worked closely with me in seminars dealing with the material presented in this book: Don Campbell, Sarah Dubin-Vaughn, Robert Gass, Frank Hayes, Lynn Knope, Derek Lawley, Gay Luce, Judith Morley, Elisabeth Rothenberger, Arnie Rowland, Margaret Rubin, Rabbi Zalman Schachter, Robin Van Doren.

I am also deeply grateful to those who helped so generously in the preparation of the final manuscript. Elisabeth Rothenberger spent many hours transcribing and organizing transcripts of several of these seminars. Caroline Whiting provided superb editorial assistance beyond the call of demand or duty. And Richard Payne, whose brilliant and creative theological mind gave valuable support and luminous insights that greatly added to my understanding of the Jesus mystery.

Sacred Journeys
and the Use of This Book

This book is one of my studies in Sacred Psychology devoted to the presentation of journeys of transformation as found in the world's great myths and stories of the soul. However ancient, these myths provide the templates for transformation and carry the coded matrices of the next steps in human development and the pattern for the partnering of human and spiritual realities.

When actively engaged, these great journeys of the soul lead you from the frustrations of the personal-particular to the fulfillment of the personal-universal with its broadening contexts and more universal formulations. You "become" St. Francis; with Percival you take on the quest for the Grail; you adventure with Odysseus; you enact the passion and the pathos of Sophia; you assume the Divine identity with Jesus. As you engage these mythic and symbolic dramas, symbolic happenings then appear in undisguised relevance to your personal story. Gradually you discover that these stories are your own stories. They bear the amplified pattern of certain rhythms and cadences in your own life. After having been Odysseus and Percival, Demeter and Persephone, Percival and Gawain, you come back to your own life enhanced and with the ability to say, "I have the strength, I have the depth, I have the capacity, the wisdom and the purpose. I will prevail." And often you do.

Since theatre and symbolic enactment provide so fundamental and effective a context for human learning and growth, sacred psychology teaches mythic stories by using drama. By engaging as participants, actors, and playwrights in profound stories of growth, challenge, wounding and transformation, as well as involving ourselves in processes that extend our own perceptual and conceptual capacities, we are seeded with a larger and deeper story. When we then live this larger story dramatically, we create the conditions and impetus for extraordinary growth. However, one should be cautioned against perceiving these mythic journeys as interesting esoteric diversions. Each of the myths in this series contains the full *agon* or journey of transformation, including the immensely potent themes of wounding and betrayal, suffering and loss, the yearning and search for the divine Beloved. In dealing with these themes we discover ways to effect the healing and resolution of those areas in our lives that have kept us caught in static anguish. By probing our own tragic dimension for its deeper story, as well as raising it to a mythic level, our wounding becomes the vehicle for grace, and we become spiritually charged and available to living a larger and nobler life. This life consummates, as we discover in all of these stories, in our seeking and finding the Beloved of the Soul, thereby partnering spiritual reality for bringing the great creative patterns of possibility into the world of space and time. Thus each offers scenarios and practices that have the effect of quite literally reweaving the tapestry of one's humanness. In agreeing to participate in these stories, you initiate a quickening in your own journey, a deepening of your own path.

This is a book to be lived and done, and not just to be read and considered. It provides an experiential journey into the life of Jesus of Nazareth and requires a courage and a willingness to participate in a power- ful adventure of the soul that is at once universal and intensely personal. Through the use of certain se- lected themes from the life of Jesus as recorded in both the orthodox and the gnostic canon of gospels, we are invited to join the personal themes of our own life to that of the universal reality informing the life of Jesus. In pursuing the Mystery Play of Jesus from his birth and baptism through his ministry and teaching, with its acts of love and grace, to his final passion, death and resurrection, we meet ourselves writ large.

The book is divided into discussion of themes and incidents from the life of Jesus, each of which is followed by experiential scenarios and exercises which allow the reader to participate dynamically in the living transformative journey of the life of Jesus. This book is especially useful for groups of people to create shared experiences as co-voyagers in the God- seed journey.

However, the scenarios and exercises can be done alone. You may want to put the exercises on tape for more convenient use. Please don't use an overly dramatic or lugubrious voice, or you'll end up not trusting the person on the tape. For those pro- cesses that require a second or a third person, you can imagine such a person or persons as being pres- ent and then dialogue with them either in journal writing or by actually playing their parts.

You will embark on the five mysteries from the life of Jesus. Groups that meet together to experience them must devote careful attention to preparing and conducting these sessions. The notes that follow are recommended as guidelines for these mythic journeys.

THE NATURE OF THE GROUP

The community that practices the journey may take any form: your family, friends, colleagues, students, clients, parishioners, etc. As the import of these experiences can be trivial or profound, it is necessary that the intention of the group and of its members be clear from the beginning. The group should consist of only those who freely choose to participate and who feel well motivated to do so. In general, the experiences should be undertaken by intelligent, resourceful people who are mature enough to have had sufficient life experience to appreciate the psychological and spiritual scope of the divine-human drama they will be required to enact.

People in community stimulate, support, and evoke each other. Their diverse reactions prime a diversity of response on the part of all. Groups also help to eradicate one of the worst tyrannies that afflicts homo sapiens: the tyranny of the dominant perception. This is reflected in such smug statements as "If it is good enough for me, it is good enough for you," and "What's sauce for the goose is sauce for the gander," and "Outside of the Church there is no truth." I do not deny the importance of consensus and commonalities but suggest instead that our differences are enriching. Thank God I need not be limited to my own experience but may share in yours. As you recognize the enormous variety and richness of the realm of the Sacred in others, you can drop simplistic judgments and stand in awe before the variety and abundance of life.

If you are able to practice the Godseed mysteries in a group, you bypass one of your greatest, and most insidious, human potentials—the potential for sloth. Self-discipline and good intentions have a way of evaporating without some consistent external commitment. The practice of Sacred Psychology, which challenges well entrenched patterns of the conscious mind, psyche, and body, needs allies. Resistance to change is natural, maybe even healthy, but the only way I know to really overcome it is through regular participation in the loving, celebrating company of co-journeyers.

Try to involve people who, in their faith in the future of humanity and the planet, are willing to work together with constancy and caring to develop and extend the Sacred in daily life. Narcissists, psychic exhibitionists, and "poor me's" may offer more challenge and distraction than you need.

In leading workshops and seminars in journeys in Sacred Psychology all over the globe, I work with diverse groups, ranging in age from fifteen to ninety-four, in education from a few years of grade school to a superfluity of Ph.D.s. Access to the Sacred seems to be as available to those whose work and external lives appear separated from the religious as to those who practice within orthodoxies. Variety has always added to the experience as culturally determined labels and expectations fall away. Be aware that, as myths have always told us, allies often come in disguise.

The group of co-voyagers for the Godseed mysteries should probably number not less than five nor more than twenty-five, although I have conducted groups of over five hundred for the entire process.

There should also be an odd number of participants, since some of the experiences are performed by couples while one member of the group is acting as Guide.

At its initial meeting the group should assign members to take responsibility for obtaining and preparing the setting or settings (indoors or out) for each of the mysteries. This includes providing appropriate music and record or tape players, art supplies, musical instruments, and other materials, as well as bringing food for closing celebrations after each session. Special attention must be taken that during the sessions there be no intruders—wandering dogs, curious children, ringing telephones. The setting is to be treated as sacred space.

As each session is built around a particular mystery from the life of Christ, it is necessary that prior to each meeting every member of the group read the relevant material from this book. The text should be read in such a way that the reader dialogues with it, taking note of images and ideas that emerge so that these may feed the group discussion. The group discussion of this material in most cases should be the subject of the first part of the meeting, so as to explore the meaning of its content in the lives and understanding of the members. The purpose of the text is only to evoke a depth reflection of psychological and spiritual patterns of transformation; it is not an occasion for theological argument. (This said, however, let me offer the following caveat. In recreating the mysteries of the life of Jesus, we are not doing so horizontally and factually, but rather vertically and mythically. We view it not as empirical data to be plotted and graphed, but as a series of mysteries to be done and danced and encountered in our depths—a living metaphor of human transformation. Thus the

reader is gently warned not to become too preoc-
cupied with the correctness of historical or theological details, as that is not what the Godseed journey is about. Some students will agree with the
perspectives offered here, others will not. The meta-
phoric mode demands a symbolic and dramatic use of
both the historical and theological material, and
when these are treated mythically and dramatically,
they gain in usefulness and creative energy what they
may lose in theological rectitude.)

After the discussion has ended, there should be a
break of at least fifteen minutes before the group
comes back together to share the mystery of the particular stage of the Godseed journey that has been
reached. A good way to do this is to leave the space in
which the discussion was held and re-enter it after a
while as sacred space—silently, with full awareness
of a commitment to making the journey meaningful.
Members of the group will spend some time center-
ing and bringing their consciousness to an awareness
of the experience about to be undertaken. Each
should make a commitment to take responsibility for
himself or herself, and at the same time respect the
needs of others and of the group as a whole.

THE GUIDE

The role of the guide is critical. This role may be held
by one person, or it may alternate among members of
the community. In any case, the guide needs to be
thoroughly familiar with the material, attentive to the
timing of the group, and respectful of the experience`
of everyone in the group. The guide is not to interpret
the experience of others but rather to trust the pro-

cess and the enormous individual variations that are possible. The group of co-journeyers must avoid the error that guide equals leader. The role of the guide, to be understood by everyone, is that of one who assists, one who enables. The role of the Guide is a most ancient one, and found one of its most accomplished forms in the hierophants of the ancient mysteries. In this tradition the guide is the midwife of the soul, the evocateur of growth and transformation. In becoming guide, then, one knows oneself to be part of a continuity stretching across millennia. In guiding these modern mysteries of the life of Jesus, the guide takes on a role of the greatest challenge and responsibility, and therefore invests it with High Self.

The guide needs to have the capacity to be at once part of the experience and observer of the travelers' journey. He or she must be able to sensitively judge the amount of time needed for the journey (only approximate times are suggested in the text) and to use the experiences flexibly. The experiences described are not cast in stone and could probably be improved by the suggestions and additions of the group and the guide.

Before the group meeting, the guide will have read the scenario material aloud several times, sensing the nature of the journey and allowing his or her voice and timing to reflect that experience. The voice must not be intrusive, but must remain clear and in relation to the experience. Wherever music is part of the experience, the guide must rehearse his or her part, so as to carefully integrate the timing of the reading and the music with the duration of the process, knowing, however, that the timing can change depending on the experience of the group.

The guide will always have one or more "soul catchers" present. These are members of the group selected because of their sensitivity to the needs of others. Thus, even while going through the experiences themselves, a part of their consciousness will be available to help others, should this be required. However, part of helping others is in knowing when to let them alone and not intrude unnecessarily on their experience. The soul catcher can also lead the guide through the experience shortly after the group journey has ended, if the guide so desires.

OTHER CONSIDERATIONS

In working with this material it is important that members of the group not take the role of therapist or theologian, and caution all involved against doing so. Professional therapists and theologians may find this very difficult, but it is imperative that they practice their profession only during regular working hours. Comments which have been heard despite repeated injunctions to refrain from making them include, "You really are blocked," or "I can see some enormous anger stored up there," or even "You really are spiritually immature." Such comments are inappropriate here, and probably don't belong anywhere. Acceptance of people for who and what they are is critical to the practice of Sacred Psychology. Each person is perfectly capable of interpreting his or her own experience and can invite the comments of others if desired.

After the experience is over, you may take some time for private reflection and recording of your experience. The understanding of Sacred Psychology and of the Journey of Jesus will deepen as you keep a journal, recording your experiences in drawings, musings, quotes, questions, and whatever else asks to be written down. This kind of expression will engage you in the most fascinating kind of conversation there is — the conversation with the inhabitants of your own inner crew.

Reflections on the experience may be shared with one or two others, or, if the group is small enough, with the group as a whole. While some may feel reluctant to share in this way, I have found that the process of verbal sharing deepens the experience for all concerned, so a situation that allows for maximum expression and participation should be encouraged.

OF TIME AND THE MYSTERIES

The entire Godseed journey with its stages of five mysteries can be performed over different time periods—even over the period of a very long day. Some may find this too compacted and intense, but others have found this condensed sequence extremely powerful because of the immediate continuity it provides for all the stages in the mysteries of the Godseed. I personally have found it best to incorporate the discussion and experiences of this book in a three to four day period, preferably during a weekend. However, they can be used an evening a week for five weeks, or according to whatever schedule works best for all concerned.

While this book stands alone as an introduction to mythic journeys of transformation, it can be used in conjunction with my book *The Search For the Beloved: Journeys in Sacred Psychology*. This work contains substantive discussions of the background, both ancient and modern, for Sacred Psychology and suggests the psychospiritual assumptions and mythic structure from which its practice flows. It also offers basic exercises designed to attune the mind and body to the work of Sacred Psychology as well as presenting several other experientially based mythic journeys of transformation.

The list of suggested music, as well as the books mentioned in footnotes, will also enhance your understanding and experience of the journey of the Godseed.

The Mystery Play of Jesus of Nazareth

JESUS CHRIST SUPER STAR

Consider Yeshua ben Yussef. A carpenter and itinerant teacher, born into abject poverty within an insignificant state at the outer edge of the Roman Empire, he lived in obscurity and died in scandal. Yet somehow this man became the spiritual cornerstone of the Western world, the central character in a first-century drama of incarnation and redemption that profoundly and mysteriously integrated all that is personal, individual and subjective with all that is historic, communal and universal.

His life was high theater, and as such both sacred and profane. It was a mystery play with ultimate and immediate human consequences. It was theater as transformational experience, as ritual, as liturgy. It was a reenactment of the full human story in the story of a human. The crucifixion provided high tragedy; the resurrection was high comedy. Together they gave Christianity a powerful drama that created a universal *therapeia* and a universal shift in consciousness. That shift was felt with fear and trembling. Of course its instigator had to be killed.

The story of Jesus of Nazareth met the full demand for paradox inherent in our human nature. It was a coincidence of the polarities — of the actual existential and the ideal essential, the myths of time and eternity, the human as potential and as realized being.

Clement of Alexandria, the Greek scholar and early Christian theologian, built his case for a universal Christianity on the fulfillment by Jesus Christ of the demands of local history and of the rising spirit of universality. Clement saw Jesus as the long-awaited Messiah, the suffering servant of the House of David whose coming had been prophesied for generations: Christianity therefore embodied the yearning of Jewish history and the Jewish people.

In addition to being perceived as the historical fulfillment of Judaism, Jesus also met the requirements of the Mystery religions: he was a man-god who died for his people. An Alexandrian Greek, Clement knew the Mysteries and had probably participated in the rites of Isis and Osiris or was acquainted with people who had. Many of you reading this book would have been involved in Mystery rites —if you had lived 2,000 years ago. Such rites included sophisticated symbolic studies, psychological purification and psychospiritual practices, as well as the physical enactment of a ritual drama in which the initiate joined the god in his or her passion and death, and then resurrected with the god into a new self and a higher meaning. In taking on many dimensions of the god archetype, the initiate engaged a larger mythos, a deeper story, a more transcendent transformation.

For Clement, and for his much greater disciple,

the philosopher Origen, Christianity was uniquely democratic: it gave to everyone what the Mysteries gave only to an elite few.[1] Furthermore, though rich in philosophic and symbolic power, the Mystery rites lacked historical grounding, since none of their chief archetypes ever lived. No Demeter or Persephone or Isis or Osiris or Orpheus was ever known in human form. One of the problems, then, with the Mystery traditions was their identification with an archetype rather than with an actual human being. There is something powerful and appealing about a personality with human proclivities (admittedly very good ones), who is contained in human skin and skeleton and organs incorporated in space and time. The classical archetypes of the Mystery traditions simply lacked the juiciness, greenness and eros necessary to sustain people in the cosmopolitan and ecumenical age of the Roman Empire. (Ironically, now that Jesus, the historical being, has become archetypal, he seems to have many of the same problems as the gods of the ancient Mysteries. After a hiatus of 2,000 years, he has, for many, become frozen in "once upon a time," and no longer enjoys the sense of vigorous aliveness that made him unique.)

So an actual historical being, Yeshua ben Yussef, feeling himself strongly identified with the ultimate archetype, God, allowed himself as man-god to be sacrificed on a tree, the traditional place for high offering in many ancient religious and Mystery traditions. He was also killed for a specific cultural reason: he claimed to be the Messiah. Thus he became the historical consummation of all the Hebraic martyr-prophets. But there was also a universal and perennial significance in the event: he was slain that, by voluntarily accepted sacrifice, he might save others. Two causalities met here: one individual and national, the other collective and universal; one the Jewish political tragedy, the other the divine need of humankind, and indeed of all life, for redemption, for transformation to a higher level of being. (See Figure 1.)

Today the same story is again being enacted. A universal, multi-national tragedy is being played out across the breadth of present spacetime. And with it comes a need for universal species redemption. We will be equal to the requirements and the response-abilities of the late twentieth and twenty-first centuries only if we have partnered the Depths. And that is why many of you find yourselves embarking on curious quests, reading odd books like this one, attending strange seminars and acquiring impractical friends.

As you can see from the diagram in Figure 1, the full meaning of the Cross *is* universal species redemption. As Clement claimed, Christianity is the true and full Mystery — and so the realized Christian is potentially the final and full being. An actual human being, Jesus of Nazareth, had fulfilled the demand of the Law and the Prophets, of the tradition and the archetype; therefore, said the Church, in this sign of the Man on the Tree, we have conquered. When the mythic structures resonant with the ancient Mystery traditions become actual and historical, the penetration into a deeper level of consciousness is extraordinary. Suddenly the Depths rise and the membrane between the worlds shatters.

In Jesus, then, were fulfilled the requirements of existential space and time and the depth needs of resurrection into eternal life and eternal time. Through this man-god one could die to one's little, local, historically conditioned self and be reborn to something wonderful. The intensity and depth of

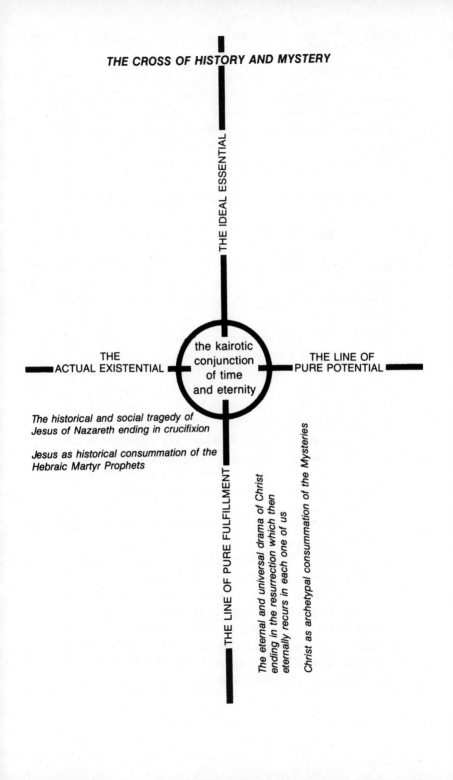

THE CROSS OF HISTORY AND MYSTERY

THE IDEAL ESSENTIAL

THE ACTUAL EXISTENTIAL

the kairotic conjunction of time and eternity

THE LINE OF PURE POTENTIAL

The historical and social tragedy of Jesus of Nazareth ending in crucifixion

Jesus as historical consummation of the Hebraic Martyr Prophets

THE LINE OF PURE FULFILLMENT

The eternal and universal drama of Christ ending in the resurrection which then eternally recurs in each one of us

Christ as archetypal consummation of the Mysteries

Christ's fulfillment of these needs explain why he became the Messiah — even though he was only one of many people alive at that time who were *entheosiastic,* filled with the God, with a Messianic consciousness at a time when everyone was looking for the Messiah.

If you had frequented the coffeehouses in Jerusalem during the time of Jesus (only they would have been winehouses), you would have heard: "Have you heard about the Messiah?" "I hear there's a Messiah down there in Caesarea. Do you think there's a Messiah there?" "Oh yes, I think there's a Messiah there." "I will lay you five to one there's no Messiah down there. There's a Messiah up in Samaria. That's the real Messiah."

When the myth, which traditionally never was but is always happening, suddenly *is* happening, then, by the sheer shock of shattering its mythic, archetypal base, it penetrates into a much deeper level of consciousness. It is as if the doors between the worlds are suddenly blown open, albeit briefly.

Many of you are preparing yourselves, whether you like it or not, for a time and place, which may be now, when the doors between the worlds *are* blown open. You don't want to stand stuttering before eternity. Many of you realize that we are in *kairotic* times (*Kairos:* loaded time, eros, passion. *Kairotic:* the passionate quality of the loaded time, when the doors between the worlds shatter.). Why now? Because of planetization. Because of the rise of women into full partnership. Because of the new technology. Because of the new physics, biology, science and the arts of consciousness in which transcendence becomes transparent to meaning. Because of the revolution in the understanding of cultures and consciousness. Because the *Zeit* is getting *Geisty.*

So at this time of thickening and intensification we say: "Where is He?" "When's She going to come?" "E.T., phone home!" "Flying saucers, we're ready for you!" We are waiting on the edge of history for someone or something special to deliver us from God knows what to God knows whom. But the old Christic demand haunts us, yelling down the years, "Yooohooo. You are it!"

"No, not me," we scream back.

"Yes, you. The things I do, you shall do, but better. You are the sons and daughters of God. You bear the promise."

"No, only you."

"No, my friend, you are it."

The entire saga of Jesus of Nazareth is full of deep psychological power. The consummation of all the symbolic forces of the human unconscious up to that time, the story begins with immaculacy, which is the symbol of an absolute opportunity. Suddenly, for whatever reason, everything is available. It doesn't last long, but it's there. Don't fritter it away then; don't talk it away. Because at that point everything becomes possible. Sudden immaculacy comes to each one of us at least several times in our lives.

The star shines into a stable. And it guides the shepherds, those with simple instincts, and the wise men, those with depth insights, to worship an infant. There, encased in flesh and lying in a stall is the divine child. The animals chew their grasses and look benignly on. What an incredible series of images revealing a clear symbolism! The wise recognize in the vast potentiality of the wholly innocent child a wisdom greater than theirs, and so they offer this infant gifts fit for a priest-king: myrrh, frankincense, and gold; the sweet-smelling aromatics of life, and the precious metal of empowerment and acceptance.

What would your life be like if, when you were two hours old, there came around your crib fascinating beings dressed in all the accoutrements of mystery and magic, offering you glinting gold and sweet-smelling things to enchant your baby mind, as well as blessing and cherishing you as the fulfillment of a promise? Stars flicker in the heavens and lovely cows with their rich, earthy smell chew happily away, their large, soulful eyes filled with great contentment. What an extraordinary beginning and coding for one's life!

While I was working on these pages, I had the wonderful experience of guiding my secretary in the last weeks of her pregnancy. Using trance and guided imagery, I told her that the initial contractions of her delivery would be felt as contractions, but then the release would be ecstatic and joyful, and she would know that she was giving birth to the Holy Child. I told her that she would experience the birth as pure pleasure and would be saying throughout the labor, "Welcome, I love you," sending abundant love to her emerging Holy Child. Shortly after having her baby she called me up and said, "I just gave birth to this little boy, and I could not believe that there was so much ecstasy in the world. I felt no pain; it was pure pleasure, for I gave birth to Holiness, you see."

The mystic child is also the son of a king, the promised Prince of Peace, but his royal descent is not recognized except by the king of violence, Herod, who tries in vain to have the true heir murdered. I have noted with interest that at this time when child abuse and family violence abound, many inner children—ones within our beings—are trying to be born. We are living in a time of spiritual gestation, when holiness, or wholeness, is trying to emerge. And the Herods within us and among us are rising at the same time. The principle of homeostasis shouts, "No! Kill the child before it's too late, or else my kingly reign of ego will be ended."

In his attempt to have the true heir murdered, Herod slaughters every Jewish male child under two years old. Scholars have speculated about the veracity of this story; it is likely that Roman law at that time would have forbidden such mass murder. The story may have been included in the scriptural narrative because it is part of a classic mythic pattern found in many child redeemer stories throughout the world. It is certainly present in every child redeemer story within every family. In any event, to avoid annihilation, the baby Jesus is spirited away. And so the classic infancy cycle closes with the child being carried off into Egypt, the place that is symbolic of the depth world and of the Mysteries.

I have frequently noticed in families, even very loving families, that when a certain child, often under the age of two, shows too much joy or exuberance, a Herod rises in one of the parents or the brothers or sisters and attempts a kind of unconscious violence. This Herod factor runs very deep. For example, when I was four or five years old and my own little brother was a tiny baby, I couldn't believe his laughter and exuberance. I knew how hard it was out there in the world. How could he be so full of innocent laughter? And just for a second I felt impelled to twist his arm. Nobody would know. And then I stopped; I didn't twist his arm. But the impetus was there, and I've always remembered it with shock and horror. Is that sort of impetus familiar to you? It is the Herod Factor. And because the Holy Child is presently being nurtured with such vitality, the intensity of the Herod Factor is rising.

The second phase of the story opens with the

agon, the ministry or journey. Mighty works are done, works of charity and of healing, of exorcism and the challenging of false, corrupt teachers; the inner core of apostles is picked and trained, and the secret of the Teacher's identity is revealed in strict confidence. This confidence is broken by one who betrays the Master to his enemies. The third phase begins with a *Pathos;* the priest-victim-hero is taken to a hill, there to die on a tree. Taken down and placed in a rock tomb, three days later he rises from the dead. This is the *anagnorisis*, the full recognition, the resurrection. Thus the cycle of *agon, pathos* and *anagnorisis* follows the stages of all classical Greek tragedies, which themselves are rooted in the cycles of classical mythic form. The cycle is thereby completed in its movement from invisibility in the womb, through the whole range of the visible, to invisibility again in the dark cave of death; from the dark stable, the entrance from the hidden, to the dark tomb, the exit from the seen. But he who enters in the apparent weakness of the immaculate Holy Child departs in the strength of complete manifestation of full maturity. And that which was apparently dead transcends itself in the fullness of new life.

We enter life in the immaculacy of pure potentiality, which we seem to lose by yards and win back by inches' on our life's journey. And then at some point we die to a part of ourselves — and suddenly out of that death we experience a resurrection, a harvest of everything we were and are and shall be, literally raised to a whole new dimension of being. Each of us has died at some point, emotionally or spiritually. And each of us can experience that death transfigured by a new pattern and a new potency.

The Christ figure, then, is an epitome of fulfillment. He fulfills the three stages of the Promise, for as the immaculate infant, he promises the redemption and new birth of the psyche. As the Prophet, he preaches repentance, conversion, or *metanoia*, which is a quantum leap of brain and mind change, a return to the Deep Ways, a rousing of consciousness, and a revelation of mighty works that authenticate the Christ nature. But he also freely offers the gift of the Christ nature to others. "These things that I do, you shall do also."

Finally, as the Priest-King, he dies for others, and rising again, conveys his grace to all who choose to become members of his mystical body. The story is powerful and primal and has unlocked levels of the deep psyche for many, whether or not they recognized it. It produces an intense force, which in turn seems to produce a kind of mutation in consciousness. The point is not whether the story ever happened; the point is that the story itself is so powerful that it releases a multitude of psychogenetic codings in human beings and activates a variety of spiritual possibilities.

How can we characterize the *kerygma* or teaching that produces such a shift in consciousness? Trained and constituted in Jewish faith and thought, Christ seems to have had in mind a re-formation, not a replacement, of Judaism. Indeed, it seems that the nature of being Jewish is to live in a state of constant renewal and reform. Christ's point of view is clearly revealed in Matthew 5:17-19, in the Sermon on the Mount:

> Think not that I have come to abolish the law and the prophets; I have not come to abolish them but to fulfill them. For truly, I say to you, till heaven and earth pass away, not an iota, not a dot, will pass from the law until all is accomplished. Whoever then relaxes one of the least of these commandments and teaches others so, shall be called least in the Kingdom of Heaven, but

who does them and teaches them shall be called great
in the Kingdom of Heaven.

The Kingdom of Heaven, or the Kingdom of
God, seems to be synonymous with the Depth World
within, a point emphasized not only in Luke, but also
in many of the gnostic gospels. To say that the Kingdom is within is a radical change in psycho-spiritual
knowing, especially in certain aspects of the more
legalistic Judaism of Christ's day. The Hebrew Deca-
logue, for example, is filled with commandments and
dictums that present God as the King who decrees
how people shall live. That stance was not true of the
depth level of Judaism then or now, but legalism is
always the temptation of religions in virtually all
times and places as one tries to make oneself accept-
able to God.

Now watch what Jesus does. In a particularly
ironic passage, he responds skillfully to a lawyer's
question, never violating the ancient Hebraic structure for formulating truth. Matthew 22:35-40 reads:

> "Teacher, which is the greatest commandment in the
> law?" And he said to him, "You shall love the Lord
> your God with all your heart, with all your soul, and
> with all your mind. This is the great and the first com-
> mandment. And the second is like it, You shall love
> your neighbor as yourself. On these two command-
> ments depend all the law and the prophets."

Love, not legalism, is the essential element of deep
spirituality. Christ's renewal of religion is based on a
dynamic reciprocity between God and human
beings—in what approximates a Hebraic form of
bhakti yoga. According to Jesus, God's love consists
of an immense yearning for human beings as persons, not as nations or peoples. Even though this
attitude has its roots in the Old Testament, it is a

radical break from a certain type of Judaic theology. The Prophets in their maturity saw God as universal and as love in action, as exercising loving dominion over all nations, not just the Hebrews. This point of view is especially clear in Second Isaiah and Jonah, but such prophetic universalism was not fully accepted until it found expression in early Christianity and, of course, in a later Judaism (though not always in a later Christianity).

So in the teaching of Jesus, God's special focus on the Jewish nation and people, or on any other people or nation, disappeared from the covenant between God and human beings. Surely Jesus was reflecting the mood of the Greek and Roman world from the time of Alexander the Great (fourth century B.C.) through the time of Constantine the Great (fourth century A.D.). This age was one of widespread ecumenism when people were becoming not *polites*, members of the local *polis* or city, but *cosmopolites*, members of a larger community such as the Alexandrian or Roman Empire. The fourth century brought the beginning of tremendous demographic shifts. Galley-sailing and donkey-riding jet setters began to travel throughout the empire. With the movements of population and the subsequent loss of traditional tribal or ethnic cultures, as well as belief and support systems, people everywhere were developing a yearning for individual security and personal redemption. This yearning contrasted sharply with the mood of the past, when the ancient Hebrews, Syrians, Babylonians, Persians and Greeks believed that the function of the gods was to protect their nations. In the past, religious life had been intertwined with the political establishment and the priests, and shrines had been government supported. But as the various nations and cultures began to succumb to the *Pax Romana* and the cultural interchange of the *cosmopolites,* faith in local divinities, archetypes, ritual structures and other parochial support systems was undermined.

A similar development is occurring in our day. Among the readers of this book are surely a number of Jewish-Buddhists. Or Taoist-Marxists, or even Sufi-Tantric-Capitalists (who also tap-dance). This is the time of mix and match, for we are in a time of tremendous ecumenism—and of rising fundamentalism, which was also true in Christ's day. So much complexity and confusion, so many choices and alternatives bring the yearning for a simplistic faith with definite directives and unquestioned beliefs. But at the same time we find a climate that provides for optimum acceptance of a larger, more vital universal but personal kingdom within. Christ's radical message was that we belong to the Deeps, to God, and in this depth connection we are redeemed, reformed and resurrected to a life that is beyond all culture.

Whether we like it or not, we have been called to a life that transcends all local boundaries, a life rooted in a planetary culture. And the radical requirement that our psyches be reformed in the Depths will give us the strength and the subtlety to live skillfully in a cross-cultural, interreligious world so that we do not destroy our planet.

Some of Jesus' best-known parables graphically portray God's love for individual human beings—no matter what their social status, cultural background, or moral condition. For example, look at the delightful trilogy of parables in the fifteenth chapter of Luke. God is represented as a shepherd who cares for a hundred sheep grazing in the wilderness. When one sheep gets lost, he leaves the other ninety-nine to search for the one that has gone astray, and when he finds it, he comes back and throws a big party (Luke 15:3-7).

Next, God is represented by a woman with ten silver pieces. When she loses one, she immediately lights the lamp and sweeps the house until she recovers it. Then she calls together her neighbors and they all have a big party (Luke 15:8-10). The third parable is the well-known story of the Prodigal Son, who takes his inheritance and goes away, has a wild and woolly time of it, hits bottom, and finally returns home. The elder son, who had been a proper Jewish boy, is shocked when his father welcomes the Prodigal with great joy and a festive celebration. "Daddy," he says, "why are you doing this? Look at me. I've been such a good son. I've always stayed put and done my work. But for me you never threw a party. My brother, the bum, finally comes home, and look what you do for him! For me, nothing."

His father rebukes him by saying, "You I have with me always, but he, your brother, who was dead, is alive again, and what was lost is now found." (Luke 15:11-32)

These parables all point to the amount of freedom God has given to us human beings. Our will is never coerced, and although we may make a great many mistakes and engage in all kinds of unskilled behavior (another term for "sin"), God's love never dies. The Deeps celebrate when we finally return home. The party is always waiting.

In one of the most important expressions of the human-divine relationship, Jesus says, "Come to me all who labor and are heavy laden, and I will give you rest. Take my yoke upon you, and learn from me; for I am gentle and lowly in heart and you will find rest for your souls, for my yoke is easy and my burden is light." (Matthew 11:28-30) When you give up your resistance, you become light; you are in a state of yoga; that is, you are yoked to the Source. Jesus was apocalyptic, as were most Jewish thinkers of the time. Thus the expectation of the New Kingdom is a theme that pervades all his teachings. Much in the New Testament indicates that Christ's notion of the Kingdom is not of Kingdom Come, but of Kingdom Already Come, the Kingdom of God as a Reign of Being, a form of psychological incarnation of Spirit in the depth lives of human beings.

Because he lived in an agrarian culture, Jesus used many earthy images in his parables of the Kingdom of the Psyche. For example, he compared the Kingdom of God to a seed cast upon the ground. While men go about their affairs, the seed, of its own strength, springs up and grows to maturity. The seed planted in the human heart also contains a transformational dynamic. It is already firmly planted in you and has its own entelechy of unfolding and manifestation.

There is an innate Taoism in much of Jesus' thinking, in his belief that if we seek the Kingdom first, then everything we need will be provided. Christ's abundant use of images from nature reveals an attitude of trust and delight. "Consider the lilies of the field more beautifully arrayed than Solomon in all his glory," and yet they don't do much except just "hang out" and look beautiful. Consider the birds of the heavens, the ravens and the sparrows, fully sustained by God's care. The implication is that if men and women would choose to live with each other in the Depths, in the communion and sustenance of the Kingdom, the Kingdom that is already come, they, too, would find in nature all that they needed.

In Jesus' teaching, no one is unworthy of God's fellowship. He constantly speaks of the infinite worth of human personhood and of the need to honor each other and treat each other with grace and according to the Golden Rule. Christ shows a fascination with little children, those who bear the full genius of human personality, the ones who have not yet forgotten the Kingdom within. He is fascinated with the possibilities inherent in the disinherited, the ones who are unpatterned, who have a certain level of freedom in their unpatroned, unparented, unpatterned condition. And he seems always to be quickening the spirits of those whom society has ostracized—the publicans, the prostitutes, the tax collectors.

Look at how Christ chose his disciples, wandering about saying, "Hey you, fisherman, you want to come? Good! You there, come out of the brothel and join us. Oh, what are you? A tax collector? Come along." There are no personal interviews, no job descriptions beyond "I will make you fishers of men," and certainly no examinations or references. Jesus could never have worked for the modern corporation. His hiring procedures make one wonder whether virtually any random sample of people, given a sense of their infinite worth, would be capable of doing almost anything. There are no exceptions to the Law of Love. The Kingdom of communion and intimacy with God has clearly come, says Jesus.

The Lord's Prayer, a celebration of immense trust and serene certainty, reveals Jesus' psychology. *Our Father* indicates Christ's perception of our family kinship with God. *Which art in Heaven* seems to mean "which art in the Depths," for "heaven" in Aramaic can refer to the depths, not just to the heavens. *Hallowed be Thy Name* points to God's name itself as potent, present and powerful. *Thy Kingdom come* tells us that the Kingdom is already here in the midst of us. *Thy Will be done on Earth as it is in Heaven* means, "Let the plans and potentials of the Depth World emerge into the world of space and time." *Give us this day our daily bread* asks for abundant sustenance and nourishment. *And forgive us our trespasses as we forgive those who trespass against us* implies that we will not experience release until we release. *And lead us not into temptation, but deliver us from evil, for thine is the Kingdom and the Power and the Glory forever* tells us that all things are possible in the family of God, even the release from shadows and unskilled behaviors.

As the "Son of Man" and "the Christ," Jesus felt himself to be a channel through which God could help humankind to recognize the Kingdom that was already in their midst. Thus he could choose the oddest random sampling of folks to follow him. He could preach and teach and heal with authority. He even had the audacity, as a hometown boy in Nazareth, to read to the local yokels, whom he had grown up with, the great passage from Isaiah: "The Spirit of the Lord is upon me. For He has consecrated me to preach the good news to the poor. He has sent me to announce to the prisoners their release and to the blind the recovery of their sight. To set the downtrodden at liberty. To proclaim the year of the Lord's favor." And with that he dared to announce to his neighbors, "This passage of scripture has been fulfilled here in your hearing today." One can almost hear the jeers and laughter that must have greeted this event, and the scriptures are very honest: "He couldn't perform many miracles there."

Because Christ felt he was in union with God and was doing the will of Being itself, he was possessed with certitude and clothed with power and authority. His whole unified life cried out, "God is speaking through me. I and the Father are One." Thus his enormous moral assurance. In the Gospels we read of

his moving swiftly and easily from one moral decision to another. He calls for complete sincerity and
asks people to put their moral sensibility above all
social, legal and ceremonial demands. He scolds the
more legalistic of the Pharisees for their obsession
with compulsive ritual and ceremonial practices, for
their loss of the moral flow of things. He tells them to
concentrate on outward behavior is immoral. If your
heart is right, he says, then you can do what you
want.

Invited to an elegant reception held for him,
Jesus shocks his host by not washing his hands and
by emphasizing the cleanliness of the inner cup
rather than merely the outer cup. "Out of the heart,"
says Jesus, "are the issues of life." His is a twofold
psycho-social concern: for one's inner integrity and
for the inner health of others. Woe, says Jesus, to
anyone who hurts another at the center of his moral
being. Harming the inner integrity of another is the
greatest of crimes.

Matthew 5:43-45 expresses the great turnabout
ethic: "Ye have heard that it has been said, Thou shalt
love thy neighbor and hate thy enemy. But I say unto
you, Love your enemies, bless them that curse you,
do good to them that hate you, and pray for them
which despitefully use you and persecute you."
Christ speaks to an unqualified wholeheartedness of
other persons. Evil must be opposed with vigor, but
people must be loved unendingly, with unlimited for-
giveness. He says that if a man wants you to go with
him one mile, you go with him two; if he asks for one
coat, you give him two coats. If he strikes you on the
cheek, you turn the other cheek. You shock people by
the abundance of your being to the point that your
little local ego self is released and your own Depths
can begin to rise.

So, from this remarkable teaching arose the Church and the baroque conundrums of Christian consciousness, many of which Jesus would probably have laughed at and disowned.

The scenarios that follow are designed to help you participate in the Christmas story, in the birth of the Christ Child, and to sense the archetypes associated with the birth of Jesus of Nazareth as it also expresses in the Depth within you. Through the processes led by your guide or reader, you will relive the ancient story of the divine birth and see its connections with your life and yourself. This Child was not alive and kicking only in a manger in Bethelehem two thousand years ago; he is struggling for your attention in your life right now.

SCENARIOS FOR THE MYSTERY PLAY OF JESUS

Process One—Before the Beginning

TIME—Approximately twenty minutes

MUSIC—Deuter's "Ecstasy" or other meditative music.

THE PROCESS—The reader or guide will say:

Let us quest within the structures of sacred time. Traditionally, reliving the myth of the sacred season, be it in Greece, Egypt, or Brooklyn, has profound consequences. You forget your profane conditions, the habituations and narrowings of everyday life. The low

but solid standards of self and society are tran-
scended and you enter for a while into a larger universe, a truer ecology of being. In the telling and the
taking of the myth, you leave behind your usual time
and are symbolically and psychologically projected
into Great Time, into a paradoxical moment that cannot be measured because it has no duration. There is
a breach in time and in the surrounding world. The
inner psyche opens and a passage to the possible
human is revealed.

The Christian myth of the birth of Jesus is an
extraordinarily powerful rite of passage. Its power in
part is in the death of the old sun, the old time, the old
way of being, and the birth of a new sun, a new time, a
new way of being. It tells of the coming of the wondrous child out of the darkness of the age and the
womb and his entry into the illuminated life of Great
Time. Once this occurs, the world turns a corner.
Everything is changed, different, re-sourced. In participating in the myth of the wondrous child, you may
feel the birth of options and opportunities in you, both
remarkable and renewing. From this comes the immense power of the story, for what could be more
evocative than the child? Here is a potency deeper
than all our fears, more basic than all our condition-
ings. It is stronger than our ego constructs, a flowing
cornucopia of that which never was but is always
happening. The myth wells from depth sources in
Reality itself, and so, more than any therapy, can cut
through the existential cul-de-sacs of our ordinary
lives. Next to this, the demeanings of December—the
alcoholic jollies, the incongruous street Santas, the
rankest commercial hype—become but the Satyricon
of the season, schlock revels to be observed but not
minded.

We are going to begin before the beginning, in

the place of the Great Plan, where it was agreed that we, the Godseeds, would be sent into the world for a new dispensation, a kind of double helix of reality. One part of you is the Christos, the Evoked One, the One who knows, the Messenger. The other part is your local, existential self. Hence the mystery of the double helix of the Great Plan. Do you remember agreeing? Do you remember the double helix of what you are? It illumines our part in the mystery of life. We are ourselves, and we are the Christos.

Now close your eyes and imagine going back to a time before you agreed to come into the world, the time before the agreement to catalyze the world.

Remember this time. Was it dark? Was it warm? Did you know a lot? Did you know a little? The time before you agreed. What do you remember? Just raise your hands and tell me what you remember about it.

(Typical responses are: "total well-being and oneness"; "soft light"; "a pulsing sensation"; "music everywhere and silver light"; "a rosy crystalline light," "a glow and an abundance of love and energy.")

In this realm you agreed. You agreed to become an angel of the divine process, a spiritual enzyme falling into time to catalyze the world, to cause the world to become more complex, to develop. You were sent by God to bring to the earth the essence of God.

Process Two—The Annunciation

TIME—Fifteen to thirty minutes

MUSIC—Lyrics of "I would not dance, Lord," included in the instructions from the reader or guide. The music for the song itself should be improvised.

SCRIPTURE—Luke 1:26-38

26   *In the sixth month, the angel Gabriel was sent from God to a town of Galilee called Nazareth,*

27   *to a virgin betrothed to a man named Joseph, of the house of David, and the virgin's name was Mary.*

28   *And coming to her, he said, "Hail, favored one! The Lord is with you."*

29   *But she was greatly troubled at what was said and pondered what sort of greeting this might be.*

30   *Then the angel said to her, "Do not be afraid, Mary, for you have found favor with God.*

31   *Behold, you will conceive in your womb and bear a son, and you shall name him Jesus.*

32   *He will be great and will be called Son of the Most High, and the Lord God will give him the throne of David his father,*

33   *and he will rule over the house of Jacob forever, and of his kingdom there will be no end."*

34   *But Mary said to the angel, "How can this be, since I have no relations with a man?"*

35   *And the angel said to her in reply, "The holy Spirit will come upon you, and the power of the Most High will overshadow you. Therefore the child to be born will be called holy, the Son of God.*

36   *And, behold, Elizabeth, your relative, has also conceived a son in her old age, and this is the sixth month for her who was called barren;*

37   *for nothing will be impossible for God."*

38   *Mary said, "Behold, I am the handmaid of the Lord. May it be done to me according to your word." Then the angel departed from her.*

There is an ancient tradition that Mary danced at the Annunciation. That is what we shall do now, male and female alike, taking the divine conception into ourselves. In this dance we will feel ourselves seeded with new possibilities and potentialities. And during the dancing, I will sing lyrics written by the Blessed Mechthild of Magdeburg in the twelfth century. I will improvise the melody and I would like you to join as I sing the song over and over again.

> I would not dance, Lord, unless thou leadest me.
> Wouldst thou that I spring mightily,
> Then must thou sing for me.
> Thus will I leap into love,
> From love into knowledge,
> From knowledge into joy,
> From joy beyond all human senses.

(The song is sung over and over, first slowly, then with a quickened pace, for an extended period of time.)

Process Three—The Doubts of Joseph

TIME—Approximately thirty minutes

MUSIC—Georgia Kelly's "Seapeace" or other meditative music.

SCRIPTURE—Matthew 1:18-25

18 Now this is how the birth of Jesus Christ came about. When his mother Mary was betrothed to Joseph, but before they lived together, she was found with child through the holy Spirit.

19 Joseph her husband, since he was a righteous man,

*yet unwilling to expose her to shame, decided to divorce
her quietly.*

20   *Such was his intention when, behold, the angel of
the Lord appeared to him in a dream and said, "Joseph,
son of David, do not be afraid to take Mary your wife into
your home. For it is through the holy Spirit that this
child has been conceived in her.*

21   *She will bear a son and you are to name him Jesus,
because he will save his people from their sins."*

22   *All this took place to fulfill what the Lord had said
through the prophet:*

23   *"Behold, the virgin shall be with child and bear a
son, and they shall name him Emmanuel," which means
"God is with us."*

24   *When Joseph awoke, he did as the angel of the Lord
had commanded him and took his wife into his home.*

25   *He had no relations with her until she bore a son,
and he named him Jesus.*

This great passage about the doubts of Joseph
reveals his temptation to disown that larger reality of
which you are all a part.

Just think of the promise, the potential, the divinity in you, which you have probably disowned
over and over again because it wasn't logical, because
it didn't jibe, because it was terribly inconvenient (it
always is), because it didn't fit conventional reality,
because . . . because . . . because. . . . What could be
more embarrassing than finding yourself pregnant
with the Holy Spirit? It's a very eccentric, inconvenient thing to have happen.

Quickly I'd like you to begin sharing in twos
your "becauses." Tell each other the reasons that you
disowned your divine potential, your divine concep-

tions. Talk quickly back and forth: "because I wasn't worthy," "because of what the neighbors would say," because . . . because . . . because. (Five minutes.)

(Let the music begin at this point.)

Lying down now and closing your eyes, imagine that you are dreaming. In your dreams you see light, and into this light comes a Being of Light, a Bearer of Good News, a Resident from the Depths. This angel says to you, "Oh Child of God, fear not to take unto yourself the spiritual partnership, for that which is conceived in you is of the spiritual Reality. And this Reality, if nurtured, shall be born of you and shall help you to go beyond your unskilled behavior and bring the Godseed into the world."

(The reader can change the words to suit the group, still keeping within the spirit of the angel's message.)

And now see what the angel sees—the fulfillment and the unfolding of this Child of Promise within you.

In the next several minutes of clock time, equal to all the time you need, see and feel and know the possibilities, indeed, the future, of this Child in you, this Godseed that you are growing in the womb of your entire being, should you allow it to be nurtured and to grow and to be born into the world.

Watch your Godseed self now. Let it grow, love it, observe its unfolding, its future. Let it come into the world. Begin now. (Three minutes.)

Acknowledge that Godseed and its future. Know its future as Mary must have known the future. Stretch and sit up, ready for whatever the next part of your life will bring you.

Process Four—The Journey to Bethlehem

TIME—Thirty minutes

MUSIC—Ferde Grofe's "On the Trail" from *The Grand Canyon Suite,* or other music suggestive of a donkey rhythm.

SCRIPTURE—Luke 2:1-5

> 1   *In those days a decree went out from Caesar Augustus that the whole world should be enrolled.*
>
> 2   *This was the first enrollment, when Quirinius was governor of Syria.*
>
> 3   *So all went to be enrolled, each to his own town.*
>
> 4   *And Joseph too went up from Galilee from the town of Nazareth to Judea, to the city of David that is called Bethlehem, because he was of the house and family of David,*
>
> 5   *to be enrolled with Mary, his betrothed, who was with child.*

THE PROCESS—The reader or guide will say:

This is the taxing that invariably occurs during the great gestation periods of our lives. You may be carrying the Holy Child, be it an idea, a project, a new possibility for yourself or others, but society knows nothing of it and shows no appreciation. At such times, we tend to resent society's demands on us and its obliviousness to our holy condition. This anger and frustration can drain the inner nurturing that is taking place and cause us to miscarry. The task at this time is to keep calm, rendering unto Caesar the things that are Caesar's, and unto God the things that are God's.

In this part of the ritual, begin by picking up pen and paper and writing a series of demands with which society, family, and profession tax you. They can range from trivia to trauma, from cleaning the cat box to changing your job. Write your list of taxes clearly, putting them in the form of declarative statements like: "Get your degree!" "Make more money!" "Get married!" "Call your mother!" "Why don't you get a real job!" And then, as we journey to Bethlehem to be taxed, I will read your lists of taxes aloud. And as I read, you will be maintaining a calm and a serenity as did Mary, remaining absorbed in the promise of that which you are inwardly carrying.

(After collecting the lists of taxes, the guide will say:)

And now, rock as if you were riding on a donkey, mindful of the divine gestation. Regardless of the list of taxes you are about to hear read aloud, continue to ride on that donkey, carrying that Holy Child. Even though the voice gets louder and louder, maintain serenity, being attentive to the Holy Child within you.

(To music suggestive of a donkey rhythm, the reader will now read aloud the lists of "taxes.")

Process Five: No Room in the Inn

TIME: Approximately twenty minutes

MUSIC: The "Hell" section of Vangelis' "Heaven and Hell" or other kinds of wandering, confusing music.

SCRIPTURE: Luke 2:6-7

6   *While they were there, the time came for her to have her child,*

7   *and she gave birth to her firstborn son. She wrapped him in swaddling clothes and laid him in a manger, because there was no room for them in the inn.*

THE PROCESS—The reader or guide will say:

Arriving finally in Bethelehem, the place of sacred space and time, you discover that no one seems to recognize you. They couldn't care less. Everything goes wrong, nothing works, you are thwarted at every turn, and there is no place to stay.

(Music begins here.)

Now begin to wander about, moving together in circles and mazes, stopping to ask each other, "Do you have room in the inn?" Those asked will answer, "No!" Continue wandering and asking for some time "Do you have room in the inn?" "Don't you have any room in the inn?" Eventually you will sense it is time to enact your own finding of the manger. You are desperate now. The baby is about to be born. (Five minutes.)

(The music ends.)

Stop now and stand beside the person you have come to in your wandering. One of you begin to speak of your yearning. Speak of your need to find whatever or whoever it is that you are searching for— that room, that place, that person, that opportunity that could complete your life.

Now the other person speaks of whatever in his or her life always says no to others. Speak the Great No that always puts the damper on everything.

For the next several minutes one of you speaks from your yearning, and the other responds from that within which always says no. And then you will exchange roles. Begin now.

(The guide will allow about five minutes for the first exchange before announcing it is time for the partners to exchange roles. Another five minutes is given for the second exchange.)

Process Six—The Birthing and the Dancing Star

TIME—Twenty to thirty minutes

MUSIC—Tomita's "Snowflakes Are Dancing" or Tomita's "Kosmos," especially the section beginning with the theme from "2001" ("Thus Spake Zarathustra"), through Wagner's "Ride of the Valkyrie," and concluding again with the theme from "2001."

SCRIPTURE—Matthew 2:1-10

1   *When Jesus was born in Bethlehem of Judea, in the days of King Herod, behold, magi from the east arrived in Jerusalem,*

2   *saying, "Where is the newborn king of the Jews? We saw his star at its rising and have come to do him homage."*

3   *When King Herod heard this, he was greatly troubled, and all Jerusalem with him.*

4   *Assembling all the chief priests and the scribes of the people, he inquired of them where the Messiah was to be born.*

5   They said to him, "In Bethlehem of Judea, for thus it has been written through the prophet:

6   'And you, Bethlehem, land of Judah, are by no means least among the rulers of Judah; since from you shall come a ruler, who is to shepherd my people Israel.'"

7   Then Herod called the magi secretly and ascertained from them the time of the star's appearance.

8   He sent them to Bethlehem and said, "Go and search diligently for the child. When you have found him, bring me word, that I too may go and do him homage."

9   After their audience with the king they set out. And behold, the star that they had seen at its rising preceded them, until it came and stopped over the place where the child was.

10   They were overjoyed at seeing the star.

THE PROCESS—The reader or guide will say:

Consider the Star. It is the connection of heaven and earth, the link between your divine and your human nature. The Star is the extension of the self into the cosmic ecology, which only the wise ones recognize. Now as the music plays, begin to do a dance of the star, being mindful of the fullness that you are bringing into the world.

(The music begins and continues till the end of this section.)

Begin to circle with your eyes and with your whole body, circling, circling, coming to feel a sense of being a star. (Pause.)

Continue to circle with your eyes, circling around inside your head, circling up and up and up, all the way up into space. (Pause.) Move further up into space, creating circles with your eyes and with your body, circles that form a funnel of energy that could snare the moon and the stars, the stars with their infinite wisdom. (Pause.)

Your body dances and circles, as your eyes circle, circling all the way up and up and up. Be mindful of the fullness that you are bringing into the world. (Pause.) When you have reached that star, circle with your eyes down, down, down into your head, down into the center of your body. Then circle with your eyes up, up, up to that star. Bring the star down, down, down, carrying it down as you circle down and down and down. Circle on your feet and with your eyes, and carry the star into the center of your being. (The guide can repeat the above or give variations on it, always speaking so as to enhance the quality of the circling process.)

Then with your eyes circle up and up and up. Circle out, out through the stars, out through the galaxies, capturing and gaining the essence of the new being, the Star Child, who is entering into time. (Pause.)

Continue circling on your feet and with your eyes, down, down, down into your very center. Holding your center, feel that star in yourself. Still circling on your feet, be aware of that star turning deep within you. Now sit down quietly. Take the star into yourself. Meditate on it as it grows brighter and brighter within you, bridging heaven and earth, inside and outside, banishing ignorance, lighting up the darkness. The star grows brighter and brighter within you. The light so rises and radiates from you that you do not know any more whether you are shined upon or are the shining one. Now becoming the star-seeded one, become stargate to an enormous universe. (Five minutes.)

Process Seven—The Wise Ones Observe the Star Child

TIME—Approximately twenty minutes

MUSIC—Alan Hovhaness, *The Mysterious Mountain.*

SCRIPTURE—Matthew 2:11

> *11 and on entering the house they saw the child with Mary his mother. They prostrated themselves and did him homage. Then they opened their treasures and offered him gifts of gold, frankincense, and myrrh.*

THE PROCESS—The reader or guide will say:

The East, the place of old wisdom, recognizes you and gives you gifts of its ancient knowings. In this part of the journey, the archaic wisdom of your own psychic deeps opens its treasures.

Sit opposite a partner now and come to silence. Let one of you be the Wise One, the Empowerer, who speaks only from the great wisdom, the deep, ancient knowings of the East, that is, from the deepest part of yourself. From those depths, speak this wisdom with wonder and astonishment at what you know and see in the Holy Child, in the other. Give to him or her your gifts of insight.

Decide now who is the first Holy Child and who is the first Wise One. You who are the Holy Child, receive your gifts deeply.

Begin now. (Five minutes.)

You who are the Holy Child, look into the Wise One's face. Gradually see the Wise One taking on the face of the Holy Child, becoming the Holy Child. You who were the Wise One, look at the Holy Child as he or she grows older. See in the face of the Holy Child the Wise One. You who were the Child, become the Wise One. Now the new Wise One speaks his or her insight, empowerment, wisdom, wonder and astonishment at what is known and seen in the other, the Holy Child. The Holy Child listens and receives deeply. (Five minutes.)

Now knowing yourself as Wise One and as Holy Child, hold and cradle with your arms that which is the best and most beautiful essence of yourself. Acknowledge and celebrate its reality.

Process Eight—The Celebration of the Shepherds

TIME—Approximately twenty minutes

MUSIC—A sampling of traditional Christmas carols.

SCRIPTURE—Luke 2:8-18

8   Now there were shepherds in that region living in the fields and keeping the night watch over their flock.

9   The angel of the Lord appeared to them and the glory of the Lord shone around them, and they were struck with great fear.

10   The angel said to them, "Do not be afraid; for behold, I proclaim to you good news of great joy that will be for all the people.

11   For today in the city of David a savior has been born for you who is Messiah and Lord.

12   *And this will be a sign for you: you will find an infant wrapped in swaddling clothes and lying in a manger."*

13   *And suddenly there was a multitude of the heavenly host with the angel, praising God and saying:*

14   *"Glory to God in the highest and on earth peace to those on whom his favor rests."*

15   *When the angels went away from them to heaven, the shepherds said to one another, "Let us go, then, to Bethlehem to see this thing that has taken place, which the Lord has made known to us."*

16   *So they went in haste and found Mary and Joseph, and the infant lying in the manger.*

17   *When they saw this, they made known the message that had been told them about this child.*

18   *All who heard it were amazed by what had been told them by the shepherds.*

THE PROCESS—The reader or guide will say:

After wisdom comes simplicity. Let us gather together like the shepherds. After the celebration of the Holy Child, the earthiness and simplicity in yourself accepts the glorious event, the birth of your own divine being. Having known the story—from the darkness of the womb to the living of the gestation, the nurturing, to the finding of a birth place in spite of all the nay saying in the world, to the taking in of the Holy Star, to the empowerment of the East and of the Deeps—let us know that we are born anew. And with that birth we are ready to live a life of new being, one that develops an extended body, an amplified mind, a compassionate heart, a deepened soul, and a

new life of high service to the God-in-Hiding, however it may appear.

So let us sing a few simple, traditional Christmas
carols together.

Merry Christmas!

NOTES

1. This perspective on the uniqueness of Christianity is
   found largely throughout two of Clement of Alexandria's major works: *Protrepticus* [Exhortations], and
   Stromateis [Carpet-Bags or Miscellanies].

The Mystery of Identity

How do you realize, in everyday life, your essential identity with God, with the One? This realization is at the heart of the Mystery Play of the life and teachings of Jesus of Nazareth. In India and other Eastern countries when someone says, "God and I are one," everyone responds, "Good for you! It's about time you finally realized that." But in the West we are shocked and clamor for the idiot to be put to death.

The story of Jesus and his mystery teaching about our divine unity has been compounded in complexity by the messianic question. Jesus appeared on the world scene at a time of enormous messianic expectation. Virgil had predicted the coming of a world savior in 10 B.C. in the Fourth Ecologue of the *Aenead*. The Jews were expecting the imminent arrival of the predicted military messiah born from the house of David, the one who would finally restore the Kingdom and free the Jews from the Roman yoke. Other nations at that time had similar messianic expectations. If the sixth century B.C. was the time of the Illumined Ones—Zoroaster, Buddha, Mahavira, Lao Tsu, Confucius, Pythagoras—then the first and second centuries A.D. were the time of the expectation of the Messiah. There is no question that Jesus, a Galilean, was raised on messianic expectations. Galilee means "circle of the Gentiles" and denotes the very large Syro-Phoenecian, Greek and Arabic populations living there. Not only were the Jews anticipating a messiah; the Gentiles were also expecting a savior.

In the famous forty-day fast in the desert, Jesus appears to have experienced a catharsis of his traditional messianism. He evidently ate nothing, drank little, and had only the creatures of the desert for companions. In other words, he was in a classical sensory deprivation situation. My own research, as well as the work of other researchers, shows that people who are placed for periods of time in sensory deprivation chambers usually project visions, sounds, and other sensory phenomena that simply do not exist in exterior reality. After a while they may even have visual and auditory projections of the issues and problems that are on their minds, occasionally seeing them symbolized as mythic or archetypal encounters. Jesus may have had a similar experience, for the gospels report that a devil came to him and offered him the kingdoms of the world and a traditional messianic role. Part of his catharsis was to get rid of his own cultural conditioning regarding traditional expectations so that he could say, "Get thee behind me, Satan. My kingdom is not of this world."

After the forty-day fast, Jesus returned to the world and worked to actively destroy the Messianic expectations of the day and supplant them with the idea that God dwells in every person, that one discovers the fullness of being within.

The whole notion of coming to fulfill a tradition and then to destroy it is a classical Western form. Many of our great philosophers followed this pattern.

Socrates came to fulfill the philosophical school of the
Sophists and instead destroyed it with his dialectical
inquiry. Nietzsche came to fulfill a certain strain of
classicism and reconstructed it beyond all recognition. Marx came to extend Hegel and instead turned
him upside down. Jesus, the rabbi, came to fulfill the
law and the prophets and proceeded to cause a
schism that the world may never hear the end of.

Christ taught that the indwelling God—as God-
Son, Logos, Christ, or Chalice of Life—is the unique
expression within us of the universal parent-being.
The term "Christ" is the critical one here, for it means
the anointed one, the evoked one, the one who real-
izes who he or she really is. It is noteworthy that
Christos and *Chrestos* were sometimes used inter-
changeably by the early Christians. *Chrestos* carries
the connotation of simpleton, great silly, or blessed
one. In one of the great apocryphal traditions, Pon-
tius Pilate is supposed to have said to Jesus, "*Ain
Chrestos!*" or "You are the fool. You are a great silly.
How can such a simple fellow create so much of a
problem?" In the necessary and natural play between
Christos, the anointed one, and *Chrestos*, the fool,
there is considerable wisdom. The one who is simple
on the surface can allow the Deeps to rise.

Jesus' concern with the indwelling of God is particularly evident in the gnostic gospels, which, far
more than the standard canon, deal with probing the
depths, going beyond historical messiahship to essential god-identity. Certain of the gnostic writings
have been known for centuries, but it was only very
recently that sufficient numbers of them were discovered and translated to reveal a picture of Jesus
that is somewhat different from the one in the
orthodox canon.

In December of 1945 near the Egyptian town of

Nag Hammadi, an Arab peasant discovered a red earthenware jar containing thirteen papyrus books bound in leather. The peasant brought them home, and his mother proceeded to use some of the papyrus sheets to kindle her fire. After a checkered history involving smuggling, black-marketeering, murder and general mayhem, ten and a half of these codices found their way to the Coptic Museum in Cairo, while the thirteenth codex was bought by the Jung Foundation in Zurich.

Translation of these second- to fourth-century manuscripts began, many of which dated from a still earlier time and contained previously unknown and even "secret" gospels. Among these are the Gospel of Thomas, the Gospel of Philip, the Gospel of Truth and the Gospel to the Egyptians, as well as other writings attributed to the followers of Jesus. There were also poems, philosophical speculations, myths and treatises on magic and mystical practices. The gnostic gospels especially contained sayings that were known from the New Testament but were presented in such a different context as to suggest new and different meanings.

So surprising were some of these discoveries to orthodox sensibilities that an aura of erudite secrecy surrounded the place of translation. I will never forget when travelling and doing a little archaeology in Egypt in the early 1970s, I was invited to visit the site where some of the translation was going on. An elderly scholar with a face that matched the patina of the papyrus showed me a shred and whispered, "Do you know what this is? Do you know what this says?" "What, what?" I whispered back hopefully, my heart speeding with excitement. After a prolonged silence he hooted, "I can't tell you." Eventually, however, a photographic series of the texts were placed in the public domain, the translations were published, and the rethinking of Jesus began.[1]

Elaine Pagels, a brilliant young scholar of early Christian writings, became one of the translators and in 1979 published a fascinating study, *The Gnostic Gospels*, which explored the radical implications of this gnostic literature.[2] Her remarkable insights blew the whistle on traditional points of view, and she was heavily criticized by those who had opted for scholarly reticence. In his *Jung and the Lost Gospels* Stephan Hoeller has taken interpretation of the newer findings to a deeper level. As Jungian analyst June Singer points out in the Foreword, Dr. Hoeller throws light on the meaning and significance of the texts and brings them "out of the past and into immediate confrontation with the crucial issues we face today."[3]

What is the "secret" behind these writings? For one thing, they present a much more complex portrait of Jesus and of his relationship to his disciples. He is sometimes cranky, is frequently whimsical, honors women, and is given to philosophical musings. One of the writers, Didymos Judas Thomas, author of the Gospel of Thomas, claims to be Christ's twin brother. Imagine what that claim would do to the story of the Nativity! And, of course, Christ's relationship to Mary Magdalene is intriguing. In the Gospel of Philip we read: ". . . the companion of the [Savior is] Mary Magdalene. [But Christ loved] her more than [all] the disciples, and used to [kiss] her [often] on her mouth. The rest of [the disciples were offended] . . . they said to him, "Why do you love her more than all of us?" The Savior answered and said to them, "Why do I not love you as [I love] her?"[4]

In studying the secret gospels, we must remember that the gnostic movement represents part of

the immense movement toward spirituality that characterized the second century in Europe and the Middle East. The external form of the search was the
longing for the supernatural savior, while the internal
form was the movement toward the gnosis of inward
knowledge and revelation.

According to the gnostic manuscript *Dialogue of
the Savior,* the disciples ask Jesus, "What is the
Way? . . . What is the place to which we shall go?"
And he answers, "The place you can reach, stand
there."[5] In the Gospel of Thomas Jesus says, "There
is a light within a man of light and it lights the whole
world. If he does not shine, he is in darkness."[6] We
see in the gnostic gospels the beginning of an emana-
tionist philosophy that perceives the light of God as
an interior unfolding, a radiating Presence which in-
vites humankind to co-creation. This idea reappeared
in the writings of St. Bernard of Clairvaux and St.
Bonaventure, but diminished in importance after the
twelfth and thirteenth centuries.

Many of the gnostic gospels direct us to the
depths of each human which contain the light, the
God-self yearning to be recognized and released into
human identity. For the gnostics, theology is really
anthropology, and exploring the psyche is key to the
spiritual quest. The gnostic quest was the West's answer to what was happening on a much larger and
more thorough scale in Eastern religious and philosophical movements. In these, states of consciousness
and the depths of unconsciousness were being
mapped and worked with to an extraordinary degree,
especially in Buddhism. The Western gnostic form of
this was more yearning than science, more fascination with the depths than explicit technique. However, in recent years, a considerable affinity has
developed between gnosticism and psychotherapy,

especially the Jungian form. The reason, of course, for Jung's fascination with gnosticism is its emphasis on Christ as evocateur of the quest of each seeker. The emphasis in Paul and the edited orthodox gospels, by contrast, tend to see only Jesus himself as "the way, the truth, and the life."

The gnostics spoke to the same concern addressed by Eastern philosophers, namely, that most people are asleep and, in fact, are dwelling in a nightmare of delusions. A famous gnostic text in the Gospel of Truth known as the "Nightmare Parable" states this idea with great poignancy. Reminiscent of Buddhism in its list of the categories of suffering brought about by our stupor and ignorance of our true selves, it describes the condition of most human beings as living

> . . . as if they were sunk in sleep and found themselves in disturbing dreams. Either there is a place to go where they are fleeing, or, without strength, they come from having chased after others, or they are involved in striking blows, or they are receiving blows themselves, or they have fallen from high places, or they take off into the air though they do not even have wings. Again, sometimes [it is as] if people were murdering them, though there is no one even pursuing them, or they themselves are killing their neighbors, for they have been stained with their blood. When those who are going through all these things wake up, they see nothing, they who were in the midst of these disturbances, for they are nothing. Such is the way of those who have cast ignorance aside as sleep, leaving its works behind like a dream in the night. This is the way everyone has acted, as though asleep at the time he was ignorant. And this is the way he has come to knowledge, as if he had awakened.[7]

The gospel goes on to say that whoever remains ignorant is a creature of oblivion, who dwells in deficiency and who will never be fulfilled. In both East and West it is this quality of obliviousness that separates unrealized beings from realized ones. In a now famous story the disciples of Buddha were reputed to have asked him, "Sir, what exactly are you? Are you a God?" "No, I'm not a God," said the Buddha. "Are you an angel, then?" "No, I'm not an angel," said the Buddha. "Well, then, what are you?" "Oh, I'm just awake," said the Buddha. And, of course, Buddha means "awake."

The good news, as well as the bad news, of the gnostic gospels is that the psyche bears within itself the potential for either destruction or liberation. You do not need an external savior or messiah to liberate you. Jesus says in the Gospel of Thomas, "If you bring forth what is within you, what you bring forth will save you. If you do not bring forth what is within you, what you do not bring forth will destroy you."[8] The bad news is that what you do not bring forth will destroy you. The emphasis in the gnostic gospels is not so much on sin as we understand it but on what you don't do. It's the omission that destroys you, not the commission.

"What you do not bring forth will destroy you." We have within us this loaded coding, this matrix of knowing, and what we do not bring forth will stultify us, put us to sleep, cripple us. The new educational movement is about bringing forth the genius of every child, the genius that is usually ignored. Children become crippled, not through misbehaving but through not being allowed to become who and what they are. And the same is certainly true of our spiritual life, our psychological life, as well as our physical life. We have within us a rich mine of resources, and if we do not tap it we will fall asleep—because we cannot bear to be conscious of our sins of omission.

"Recognize," Christ says over and over again. "Recognize what is before your eyes, and what is hidden will be revealed to you."[9] But he points out the difficulty of being persistent in the face of the siren call of drunkenness and the lure of sleep. "When I came into the world," says Jesus in the Gospel of Thomas, "I found them all drunk; I found none of them thirsty. And my soul became afflicted for the sons of men, because they are blind in their hearts and do not have sight; for empty they came into this world, and empty they seek to leave this world. But for the moment they are drunk."[10]

The recognition of the awesome possibilities of spiritual discovery through exploring and entering our own depths is a key to the gnostic texts. In the Gospel of Thomas Jesus says, "Let him who seeks continue seeking until he finds. When he finds, he will become troubled. When he becomes troubled, he will be astonished, and he will rule over all things."[11]

Judging from these gospels, the key emphasis of Jesus' teaching was the quest for the Kingdom of Heaven within. Why is this emphasis lacking in orthodox Christianity? As Elaine Pagels has suggested, the answer is probably political. Because the early formal church and bishops wanted exclusive governance. Early bishops like Irenaeus, Bishop of Lyons, severely attacked the gnostic emphasis on the individual inner quest, seeing it as the ruination of the infant Church. In a sense he was probably right. "They go around puffing themselves up with their own knowledge and their own quest," he complained, and then alleged that their inventiveness and creative imagination led them to express their own insights, not necessarily those of the Church.[12]

Imagine St. Patrick's Cathedral gone wildly gnostic on Sunday morning. A woman in the front row is humming, "OMMMMM." In the aisles a man is spinning himself into ecstasy in good Sufi dervish fashion. Another man is chanting up someone's chakras, while in a corner chapel an old woman is rapt in profound Zen mediation in front of a statue of the Buddha holding the Madonna and Child on his lap. And then, of course, there is the nun dancing on a little bed of coals in front of the altar. Now if you can just multiply this (albeit exaggerated) scenario by a factor of ten, you might imagine Irenaeus' sense of horror at what was going on with the gnostics at the time. Although this variety might constitute a vital church, it would hardly be an ecclesiastical ideal.

The Christians at that time were victims of acute persecution and the major social event in Lyons seems to have been watching them be consumed by large beasts. Irenaeus had only scorn for those gnostics who went happily on their inward way, separating themselves from the suffering community of "true Christians." In fact, he regarded them as more dangerous than the dinners provided at the Roman circuses, for there only the body is consumed, while the gnostic belief obsesses the soul.

It was the formal Church of the late second and early third centuries that chose the final definitive canon of Christian gospels and writings. The gospels included were those that focused on Jesus as the only way to God, and his only line of succession derived from the apostles and their disciples, these being the only legitimate heirs of the true Church. The fact is, of course, that there were many gospels, perhaps hundreds. Judging by archaeological and philological findings, a fair number of these emphasized Jesus preaching the quest for the kingdom within, as well as the consequent identity with Godhood that is the natural, necessary correlate to living in this kingdom.

What this attitude would do to a formal church structure is apparent. If everybody is in a state of revelation, or worse, identity with God, how could you have any priests or bishops or other special hierarchical folk proclaiming the right way to live?

Most of the "unorthodox" gospels reiterate over and over the message found in the Gospel of Thomas where Jesus ridicules those who thought of the Kingdom of God in literal terms, as if it could be found in a specific locale. He says: "If those who lead you say to you, 'Look, the Kingdom is in the sky,' then the birds will arrive there before you. If they say to you, 'It is in the sea,' then the fish will arrive before you." Instead, it is a state of self-discovery:

"Rather, the Kingdom is inside of you, and it is outside of you. When you come to know yourselves, then you will be known, and you will realize that you are the sons of the living Father. But if you will not know yourselves, then you dwell in poverty, and it is you who are that poverty."[13]

When the disciples persisted in looking for the Kingdom in time, asking "When will the Kingdom come?" Jesus answered, "It will not come by waiting for it. It will not be a manner of saying 'Here it is' or 'There it is.' Rather, the Kingdom of the Father is spread out upon the earth, and men do not see it."[14]

The Kingdom, then, is a state of being, a transformed consciousness, a radical change of attitude, an *enantiodromia*, a big turnaround. In *The Irrational Season* Madeleine L'Engle suggests that experiencing the Kingdom is like visiting the most beautiful planet in the universe, but with only one sense, say touch, operating. Much can be felt and known through the sense of touch. Then suddenly we are granted a million senses with which to perceive this planet and all its beauty. That's what the Kingdom is like.

When we existed as insular, tribal, or nationalist beings, living in a survival mentality, we used only a small percentage of our inner and outer receptors. But living in the Kingdom demands that we use more and more of our physical, spiritual, mental, and emotional resources. We need to turn on all of the many receptors with which we have been so richly gifted but which we so rarely use. For unless we come to experience this planet as the Kingdom, we will have neither the energy nor the urge to save it. Experiencing new ways of knowing will evoke in us the love, commitment, and courage to partner this beautiful planet, this form of the Kingdom Already Come.

Consider Jesus' statement in the Gospel of Thomas: "When you make the two one, and when you make the inside like the outside, and the above like the below, and when you make the male and the female one and the same . . . then you will enter the Kingdom." These kinds of powerful, passionate, paradoxical knowings, expressed explicitly through most of the gnostic gospels, are veiled in the standard canon, with Kingdom Come expected in a near future as a cataclysmic social event. Only in Luke, where Jesus says with great clarity, "The Kingdom of God is within you," do we have this theme openly expressed. The Church did believe in an inner kingdom, but it also believed that something external called "Kingdom" was going to come. So the institution set itself up as a holding pattern for the interim, with interim ethics, an interim sociology, and an interim value system. And all interim measures are at best patinas; they don't supply much spirit or substance.

An interim holding pattern also keeps life on ice, and sooner or later we begin to suffer a metaphysical pathology of timing. This interim holding pattern has cast its long shadow down through the centuries, bringing with it the diseases of timing that afflict Western life—heart diseases, stress diseases, cancers. For are not many of these the result of living too long in the holding pattern rather than in the Kingdom? And when the missionaries take this pathology of metaphysical timing into Africa and South America and Asia, suddenly heart disease and cancer and stress appear in areas where they were rarely seen before. The revolutions and rising expectations of third world countries today may be the result of leaping out of the interim, of wanting the Kingdom *now*, so that a more natural timing for things to happen is lost and revolution succeeds revolution.

What would the third world be like if it existed with the notion that the Kingdom is already come, that it has to be farmed and nurtured but is already present? Perhaps the interim holding pattern imposed by the Christian colonial powers would finally be broken. For this pattern did not allow third world countries their own genius and styles of sensory, emotional, and psychological knowing to rise to the opportunities that were being presented. ("Hello there, my little brown brother. Let me show you the Christian way of doing things!") And thus the excesses of Marxism and of revolution proceed naturally from the excesses of an interim Christianity whose narrow notions of the way the interim world works inhibited the genius and integrity of so many cultures.

If we take the gnostics seriously, the interim pattern is rendered superfluous and obsolete: the Kingdom is not to come but is already in our midst. Then, suggest the gnostics, and one can hear Irenaeus shudder, the Church becomes an Ecclesia of high practice to help people reveal what is already there, and not the celebration of some once and future historical event. Not that the gnostics don't recognize the need for guidance, but they see it as only provisional and temporary, a way station on the road to spiritual fulfillment and high development.

The gnostic writings shed much light on what Jesus was evidently trying to say in the standard gospels. I have found that many people reading the gospels for the first time without the illumination of the gnostic canon have a psychological field day with Jesus. This is especially true of people in the helping professions, who are given to labeling or "diagnosis" (the psychiatric form of character assassination). They describe Jesus as either enormously crazy (paranoid, schizophrenic, obsessed with his own identity) *or* tremendously integrated (experiencing union with the God-Self).

In its great opening passage, the Gospel of John, the most gnostic of the four New Testament gospels, says that the Logos became flesh. The Logos, the divine and universal creative expression, which is eternal and lives outside of time, can be consciously enfleshed in your life. Now this Logos is not archetypal; it's deeper than any archetype. The Logos calls itself "I Am" or "I Am That I Am" or even "I Shall Be What I Shall Be." This "I" of the self-identity of God is emphatic and reiterative in ancient Hebrew literature. God says to Abraham, "Seekest thou the God of Gods? I am He. . . . I am before the days were. . . . I am before time was spun out of existence." And, in another passage, "I am not an angel; I am not a seraph; I am not the envoy; I, the Lord, I am He and no other." "I Am That I Am" is perhaps the most powerful self-expression of God.

"I" is the name of God in the great tradition, and it is the name declared by Jesus. Thus his constant statement that it is only through the "I" Being that we reach the truth of our own being. Krishna says in the *Bhagavad Gita:* "There is no past when I was not, nor you, nor these; and we/Shall-none and never-cease to live/Throughout the long-to-be."

The name of God in man, "I," is deeply buried in the human psyche. As Doris Lessing would say in some of her recent science fiction novels, it is a part of your brain print, implanted in you as an agent of the cosmos. Jesús' transformational teachings sought to elucidate this "I" and its correlate "Son of I," as well as to clarify what it means to live in the inner Kingdom of the I Am. Christ was the mighty quickener of the "I Am," the first to bring the "I Am" into its full significance. We might say that Christ's words describing the inner Kingdom run parallel to modern depth psychology's descriptions of the unconscious, although they exceed these descriptions by far. You may be familiar with Carl Jung's exploration of the archetypal realms of the inner world, as well as the personal and the collective unconscious, where so much of the vital force of any person lives. But you may not know that even Freud, in his last writings, recognized that the unconscious does not coincide with what is repressed; all that is repressed is unconscious, but not the whole of the unconscious is repressed. He saw that part of the ego is unconscious and in his last writings came to postulate a third unconscious that is not repressed. He suspected that this would prove to be the most important unconscious of all, the very foundation of psychic life. In his eightieth year he said that if he had the chance to live over again and start afresh, he would start with the third unconscious. (It is wonderful how people who are truly great geniuses can transcend their own work.) The "proto-gnostic" Freud of the later years might have proved a great embarrassment for standard psychotherapy if he had written more, and even this he addressed in the last days of his life when he said, "Thank God I am not a Freudian."

This foundation of psychic life is probably what Jesus meant by the "Son of Man," the "I" or the "Deep Self." In living as the "Son of Man," he confronted people with the power of their own inner kingdom and its capacity to transform inner and outer realities. For this Logos self is the life force of all creative and recreative power.

Just as Christ is the expression of the Logos principle, so the Sophia, frequently referred to in the gnostic gospels and writings, is the expression of the great feminine principle of Divine Wisdom. As Wisdom she appears in the early Jewish Wisdom literature (Proverbs, Wisdom of Solomon, and Ecclesiastes) as the Divine Feminine. Proverbs states that "God made the world in Wisdom," a saying taken by some interpreters to indicate Sophia's partnering of the Creation as well as her being the feminine aspect of the I Am. In the gnostic texts hers is the saving knowledge, and in her resides the whole possibility of salvation and transformation. Relationship with the Sophia provides the balance between masculine and feminine spiritual principles that the gnostic Jesus spoke of as necessary for the full development of life in the Kingdom. Later Christianity gave to Mary some of the same order of devotion and concern that the gnostics gave to the Sophia. Indeed, Mary was often treated as an incarnation of the Sophia. (In certain circles of gnostic Christianity Mary Magdalene filled this role of avatar of the Sophia. She is referred to as the "woman who knew the All.")

God-illumined folk have always spoken of the blazing union with a Reality that contains both masculine and feminine aspects of Divinity, both Logos and Sophia. Indeed, current movements in spirituality reflect a vital resurgence of theological interest in the Sophia, as well as the growth of practices and devotions around this feminine principle of spiritual identity. (There is such a practice at the end of this section.)

Many of us live in the pathos of the great divide of self and spirit. We see the men and women who have come to true identity consciousness, incarnating both the Logos and the Sophia principles, as wholly other. They serve as screens on which we project our dependencies, since we are often unwilling to do the work that allows the Godseed to flourish within us. So we choose to rest in dependency rather than responding to the radical demand such realized persons make of us—that we do as they do, and even more.

When Freud said, "What had been id must become I," he was confluent with Jesus' emphasis on the "I." The repressions, the compulsive behaviors, and the anxieties of the id-ridden psyche are transformed by virtue of joining a much larger and deeper process and presence of Identity. So Jesus says to heavy-laden, id-ridden folks, "Come unto me all ye that labor and are heavy laden and I will give you rest and you will find your souls refreshed."

As your eternal and elder Self, the "I," emerges from beneath the accumulations of your historical life, you will find yourself transformed beyond personal history. "Before Abraham was, I am." The skins of your historical and cultural selves are sloughed off, and you come into the core reality of I Am-ness which was and is and shall be. "I Am" the way out of the maze of confusion and lostness of historical existence. But as Jesus pointed out, you must lay down your local life in order to pick it up again, restored, restocked, and renewed on a higher level.

When you pick up your local self again, reconstellated by the I Am That I Am, you will not be the same flesh, much less the same self. Since the brain-mind system can change radically in the twinkling of an eye, the power of your unique destiny or entelechy can charge both the patterns as well as the protein of one's existence. This phenomenon is, as we shall see, what the mystery of resurrection is about. Yes, every cell can be renewed, refrequenced, revibrated, restored. Conscious rebirth into the local life out of the womb of the Depths is implied again and again until "Thy will be done on earth as it is in heaven," and the depth life of the I Am becomes unified with the local life. Then the Son of Man, the Purusha, the Anthropos, the coding for the next stage of humankind, is released out of the Depths. And you simply will not be the same. A before and an after will exist on opposite sides of an abyss of immeasurable dimensions. In the before you are your local self, and in the after you are I Am, *Domine*. The Lordship of Being has entered into you with the paradox that, with regard to others, in this state you are always servant and never "Lord."

As we have seen, Jesus used parables to describe the indescribable Kingdom of Heaven. It is astonishing and more than a little amusing to see how many of his words correspond to those that physicists are using today to describe the quantum nature of reality and holonomic theory. Granted, this may beg questions, but the Kingdom is nothing if not relational with all ideas and questions. So Jesus tells us: "The Realm of Heaven is like a treasure hidden in a field; the man who finds it hides it, and in his delight goes and sells all he possesses and buys that field."

Quantum physics and holonomic theory give us a picture of many different quantum fields interpenetrating each other. Each fills the whole of space and has its own particular properties. Furthermore, as Bell's theorem indicates, no theory of reality compatible with quantum theory can require spatially separated events to be independent, but must allow for the interdependence and interconnection of distant events in a way that differs from our ordinary experience. Everything interpenetrates in this field of reality. The depth world of the I Am is the source level of this matrix that is simultaneously everywhere. Therefore, to have access to the I Am mindset of the Kingdom is to experience the wholeness of all interpenetrating fields, all realities.

In another parable Jesus says that the Kingdom of Heaven is like a trader in search of fine pearls; when he finds a single pearl of great price, he goes off to sell everything he owns in order to buy it. This parable recalls the metaphors describing the very nature of Reality in the wonderful second century B.C. Buddhist Avatamska Sutra:

> In the heaven of Indra there is said to be a network of pearls, so arranged that if you look at one you see all the others reflected in it, and if you move in to any part of it, you set off the sound of bells that ring through every part of the network, through every part of reality.
>
> In the same way, each person, each object in the world, is not merely itself, but involves every other person and object and, in fact, on one level is every other person and object.[15]

This cross-cultural and cross-historical exchange of spiritual metaphors reaches its apex in Jesus' words, "The Kingdom of Heaven is like a net, which was thrown into the sea and collected fish of every sort." What is a net but a pattern of fields that collects and reflects and connects all manner of realities, as we see in the metaphor of Indra's net. These two

Eastern and Middle Eastern metaphors, offered within two centuries of each other, link the power of ancient gnosis to the modern gnostic speculations of physicists. The pearl, the net, the field, the Kingdom are metaphors of congruence and resonance such as we find in quantum and holonomic descriptions of reality. But they also exceed description and can ultimately be found only in the experience of Identity wherein you know, and you know that you know, and you become the One in the Many and the Many in the One.[16]

Process One—A Ritual of Baptism

TIME—At least thirty minutes

MATERIALS—A number of stones of various sizes to be chosen by each participant; a jug or pitcher for water (several jugs if there is a large group), some magic markers or other writing utensils that will write on stone.

SPECIAL INSTRUCTIONS—This process can be adapted to the circumstances of place, time and geography. A lake, stream or ocean is suitable. A bathtub is merely adequate.

SCRIPTURE—Matthew 3:1-17

> *1   In those days John the Baptist appeared, preaching in the desert of Judea,*
>
> *2   [and] saying, "Repent, for the kingdom of heaven is at hand!"*

3   *It was of him that the prophet Isaiah had spoken when he said:*

A voice of one crying out in the desert,
"Prepare the way of the Lord,
make straight his paths."

4   *John wore clothing made of camel's hair and had a leather belt around his waist. His food was locusts and wild honey.*

5   *At that time Jerusalem, all Judea, and the whole region around the Jordan were going out to him*

6   *and were being baptized by him in the Jordan River as they acknowledged their sins.*

7   *When he saw many of the Pharisees and Sadducees coming to his baptism, he said to them, "You brood of vipers! Who warned you to flee from the coming wrath?*

8   *Produce good fruit as evidence of your repentance.*

9   *And do not presume to say to yourselves, 'We have Abraham as our father.' For I tell you, God can raise up children to Abraham from these stones.*

10   *Even now the ax lies at the root of the trees. Therefore every tree that does not bear good fruit will be cut down and thrown into the fire.*

11   *I am baptizing you with water, for repentance, but the one who is coming after me is mightier than I. I am not worthy to carry his sandals. He will baptize you with the holy Spirit and fire.*

12   *His winnowing fan is in his hand. He will clear his threshing floor and gather his wheat into his barn, but the chaff he will burn with unquenchable fire."*

13   *Then Jesus came from Galilee to John at the Jordan to be baptized by him.*

14   *John tried to prevent him, saying, "I need to be baptized by you, and yet you are coming to me?"*

15   *Jesus said to him in reply, "Allow it now, for thus it is fitting for us to fulfill all righteousness." Then he allowed him.*

16   *After Jesus was baptized, he came up from the water and behold, the heavens were opened [for him], and he saw the Spirit of God descending like a dove [and] coming upon him.*

17   *And a voice came from the heavens, saying, "This is my beloved Son, with whom I am well pleased."*

THE PROCESS—The reader or guide will say:

This ritual releases our sins and our unskilled behaviors and baptizes us into new life. In many cultures baptism is the ancient form of entering a new period of one's life in which one agrees to be free from old and destructive habit patterns. In the story of the baptism of Jesus by John we have the clearest statement of this agreement, for with the baptism, Jesus enters the mature phase of his life and teaching. This baptism ritual is our commitment to Unitive Consciousness and it indicates our willingness to release old patterns and allow the depth of Unity to rise in us. It is our statement in ritual reality that we are willing and ready to take on the task of transformation.

In a few moments I am going to ask you to find a stone or stones on the path we will walk to the lake. Carry a pen that will write on stone. There will be time at the lake for you to write on this stone or stones those attitudes, those habits, those personal sins, those unskilled behaviors that you would like to cleanse yourself of, that you are committing yourself to be rid of.

In the culture of Jesus, writing was very important. Remember that Jesus writes in the sand when the woman is taken in adultery and is about to be stoned. He says, "He who is without sin, let him cast the first stone." As people come up ready to stone the woman, Jesus keeps on writing in the sand, and it is assumed that he is writing their particular sins and unskilled behaviors.

Sand can be smoothed over; stones will be washed in the lake. But your act is not only a cleansing and a commitment; it is also a field of resonance. The field of your cleansing goes out to the farthest star. You are engaging that cleansing field by your ritual act.

At the lake (stream, river, creek) you will stand holding your stones until all are present. I will fill a pitcher with water from the lake and pour some of the water over the head of the first person to be baptized. I will say, "Be thou baptized." The entire group will chant from the perspective of the I AM nature of God: "This is my Beloved Child in whom I am well pleased." All of you together will represent the I AM and speak these words with joy, with celebration, in full voice: "This is my Beloved Child in whom I am well pleased."

As you are being baptized, just before the water is poured on your head, drop or throw your stones into the water of the lake. After you release your stones, which are symbols of what you are cleansing yourself of, observe the patterns they make in the water. Then kneel and allow the water of baptism to flow over you as the group speaks the words of celebration.

The person just baptized will select another person and baptize him or her. And the process will be repeated until all of us have baptized and been baptized by another, have released our stones into the water and have spoken together as the I AM.

Let us walk to the lake (stream, river, creek), gathering stones as we make our way to the place of the Ritual of Baptism.

Process Two—Wandering in the Wilderness: The Temptation of Christ

TIME—Approximately forty-five minutes

SCRIPTURE: Matthew 4:1-11

1   *Then Jesus was led by the Spirit into the desert to be tempted by the devil.*

2   *He fasted for forty days and forty nights, and afterwards he was hungry.*

3   *The tempter approached and said to him, "If you are the Son of God, command that these stones become loaves of bread." He said in reply, "It is written:*
'One does not live by bread alone,
but by every word that comes forth
from the mouth of God.'"

5   *Then the devil took him to the holy city, and made him stand on the parapet of the temple,*

6   *and said to him, "If you are the Son of God, throw yourself down. For it is written:*
'He will command his angels concerning you,
and with their hands they will support you,
lest you dash your foot against a stone.'"

7   *Jesus answered him, "Again it is written, 'You shall not put the Lord, your God, to the test.'"*

8   *Then the devil took him up to a very high mountain, and showed him all the kingdoms of the world in their magnificence,*

9   *and he said to him, "All these I shall give to you, if you will prostrate yourself and worship me."*

10   *At this, Jesus said to him, "Get away, Satan! It is written:*
   'The Lord, your God, shall you worship
   and him alone shall you serve.'"

11   *Then the devil left him and, behold, angels came and ministered to him.*

THE PROCESS—The reader or guide will say:

Now begin to form dyads, working if possible with someone you do not know very well. In this process, one partner will be the speaker-witness. The other will speak as the Devil-Tempter, who tempts you as Jesus to live up to the cultural expectations of the Messiah.

The speaker-witness, taking the part of Jesus, answers the Devil as the Christ in you answers. (The speaker speaks not as the historical Jesus but as his or her own self in present time.) Pledge allegiance to a different, higher Kingdom, proclaiming, if possible, "Get thee behind me, Satan!"

The Devil seeks to be persuasive and subtle, looking for weakness in purpose, in will, in arguments. You as speaker will marshall your sense of purpose in life as well as your personal and spiritual resources in refuting the Devil's arguments, persuasions, and wiles—unless the Devil's arguments are convincing enough to change your mind.

The partners wander in the wilderness together for about twenty minutes, the devil holding the speaker's arm and whispering in his or her left ear, while the speaker refutes or agrees with the devilish arguments. Then the roles are exchanged and the wandering and tempting continue for another twenty minutes.

This practice serves to disengage you from your attachment to the cultural ego. Begin now.

Process Three—The Mantra of Identity

TIME—Twenty minutes

THE PROCESS—The reader or guide will say:

We will perform together a process that is an expression of identity. It consists of a mantra that can be sung, danced and chanted. It is a quickening of the I Am, a movement out of the local self into the Deep Self, into the Ground of Being. If you practice it every day at the beginning of your day, you will notice a movement out of local self into I Am-ness, into the Depths.

Move quickly now into groups of three. While standing, the three of you hold hands. You will begin to chant with me, picking up the rhythm of the chant as we go along. But first, listen for a moment.

On the physical plane, where is perfection? Everywhere. It is perfect. It is perfect. Where is perfection on the plane of feeling? You are loved. You are loved. When you feel that, you know it. Yes, yes, I'm loved. Ah, yes. That's perfection in the realm of feeling.

Arr. by ROGER JOYCE

Now where is perfection in the realm of the mind? All is clear. All is clear. And where is perfection in the realm of essence? I am holy. I am holy.

And now we will begin to chant "It is perfect. You are loved. All is clear. And I am holy." As we all chant "It is perfect," we will bow forward. As we all chant "You are loved," we will bow right. As we all chant "All is clear," we will bow left. And as we chant "And I am holy," we will raise arms and hands toward the heavens. Let's begin: "It is perfect. You are loved. All is clear. And I am holy." A little faster now. (The chant is repeated with the movements for about five minutes.)

Now choose one of your group to chant, "It is perfect," one to chant, "You are loved," and one to chant, "All is clear." In this next round of chanting, each of you individually will chant your particular line of the mantra, and on the fourth line, "I am holy," all three of you will chant together. Concentrate especially hard on this form of the chant. Make sure you don't go off on your own tangent or stay inside your own ego. Really collaborate and share the consciousness of this chant with the other two people in your triad. Ready? Begin now, "It is perfect. You are loved. All is clear. And I am holy." (The chant is repeated with movement for about five minutes.)

Now each triad join another triad and the six of you stand in a circle. The two people who chanted "It is perfect" stand facing each other in the circle; the two who chanted "You are loved" stand facing each other; and the two who chanted "All is clear" stand facing. Now each triad of chanters hold hands in such a way that they form a Star of David, consisting of two triangles intertwined. Just reach out with your hands, as you did with your original triad, but with your right hand over and your left hand under your neighbors' hands, so you have a strong, well-woven Star of David.

Now as a group of six, again chant the mantra. First the entire group chants each line: "It is perfect. You are loved. All is clear. And I am holy." Begin and pick up the pace as you chant. (Five minutes.)

Now the two "It is perfect" partners chant their line; then the two "You are loved" partners chant their line; then the two "All is clear" partners chant their line, then all six chant "I am holy." Begin now. (Five minutes.)

(This process is adapted from one presented in my Jesus seminar by Rabbi Zalman Schachter, a good friend and marvelous colleague, and one of the most original minds participating in the present rise of a new world spirituality.)

Process Four—The Great Spiral of Wisdom: A Visit to the Sophia

TIME—From one to eight hours (The process can be used as either a short process of guided imagery to visit the Sophia or as an all-night dream incubation. The scenarios for both processes are given here.)

MATERIALS—A drum, rhythmically struck by a drummer for the first part of the process. A copy of *The Nag Hammadi Library* if the all-night dream incubation is to occur.

THE PROCESS—The reader or guide will say:

We are going to begin to move into a reflective frame of mind, a frame of mind that will encourage us each to conceive a deep question to be asked of the Sophia, the great feminine gnostic principle of wisdom. As we move into reflection, our drummer will be striking the drum with a slow, regular rhythm.

We are now moving into remembrance of the Great Spiral of Wisdom, the Great Spiral of the Life Force. Begin now by lying on your back. Make a spiralling movement with your feet, clockwise. Let that spiralling movement move up to the ankles and the knees. Continue spiralling up to the thighs, to the buttocks, the abdomen and the torso. Then spiral up to the shoulders and the neck and the head. Continuing to make a spiralling movement clockwise. Spiral with your head. Continue to spiral down the neck,

the shoulders, the torso and abdomen, the buttocks, the thighs, the knees, down to the ankles and the feet. From the feet spiral up to the ankles, the knees, the thighs, the buttocks, the abdomen, the torso, the shoulders, the neck, the head. Then spiral down again.

Keep this spiralling going as you lie there. You should be making a lot of movement. This movement is called roiling. It is the basic movement of the DNA spiral, of the galaxies, of the unfolding of the Life Force. The Sophia requests that you make this movement for the next few minutes, for it may help you create a clearer vortex channel for the reception of Wisdom. Spiralling from the feet up to the head and back down to the feet connects you with all spirals. The spiral contains all wisdom and all information, from the coding of galaxies to the coding of molecules. As you make this great paradigmatic movement of the spiral, you recreate in yourself the pattern for the passageway of Wisdom.

Continue spiralling now. Hold your question as you spiral. Put your personal question about the meaning and possibility of your life into every part of the spiral.

Continue the spiralling, never stopping. Spiral all the way up and all the way down. Make a gentle movement from the feet up to the knees, up to the thighs, up to the buttocks, the abdomen, the torso, the shoulders, the neck, the head, and then all the way down. Make the great spiral, the great channel for Wisdom to find its path.

Continue the spiralling with your body all the way up and all the way down.

Now come to silence in your body, and the drum will now stop. (Pause.)

We are now prepared to take the journey to the Sophia. You find yourself on the foothills of the green Earth at the bottom of a Spiral Mountain. At the base of the mountain are very primitive people dressed in simple skins, Neanderthals, some with their arms full of sticks, some chipping flint stones. They greet you as you go by. Continue up the mountain, passing men and women who belong to the early Neolithic era. The women are dropping seeds into the earth after they have penetrated the ground with a sharp stick.

Continue up the mountain. Suddenly you find yourself in the great river valleys of the beginnings of high civilization: the Yangtze, the Tigris and Euphrates, the Nile. You see people reclaiming land from the swampy waters and gradually building along it, building sphinxes and pyramids and ziggurats and temples and graineries and great cities.

You continue up the Nile. You seem to come to the Mediterranean basin as you climb the mountain. You are in ancient Greece. As you continue, you are in other civilizations of the same era. You see Gautama Buddha finding enlightenment under the Bo Tree in India; Confucius giving wisdom to the courts of the Duke of Lu in China.

Still continuing up the mountain, you come to the Middle East, Persia, in the time of Alexander. Alexander the Great is marching across vast stretches of the world. Continuing up the mountain, you find yourself in a high civilization in West Africa, and then in an ornate culture in South America.

Further up, you see Jesus, whittling on a piece of wood, thinking, asking Mother Wisdom, "What is my task? What is the appropriate thing for me to do?" For he is not yet entirely aware of his I Amness and his destiny.

As you continue up the mountain, you see the legions of Rome. Then you are in the time of the Dark Ages. Next you are in the Crusades, then in the court of Kubla Khan, the Great Emperor of China.

Continuing up, you find yourself in the High Middle Ages, and great vaulted cathedrals rise in cities, and trade guilds and craft guilds—for goldsmithing and weaving and the selling of wool and spices and all kinds of products are beginning to spread.

Continuing, you see Michelangelo lying on his back painting the Sistine Chapel. You see Leonardo da Vinci attempting to fly in the strange wing-like contraption he has invented, and you are in the Renaissance.

Further up the mountain, you see Queen Elizabeth, with her great starched ruff and her great skirts and her little red wig, watching a performance of *Hamlet* at the Globe Theater in 1600. As you continue up the mountain, you see great masted ships setting out to explore new lands, both east and west.

Further on, you see the spread of a new kind of power, steam power, and chugging little trains crossing continents, India and Europe and America. You continue up the mountain and see cities spread, linked by rail and telegraph.

Next you find yourself in the twentieth century with its cars, trains, planes, telephones. Continuing up the mountain, you arrive in the age of high technology, and the world is linked by telecommunications. Somewhere there is a mushroom cloud, and you see nuclear reactors. As you continue, it seems that at the top of the mountain you are at the present moment. But then you go inside the mountain to a path that travels downward in a spiral. Moving along the path down and around within the inner mountain spiral, you pass scenes of your own life, from your earliest infancy. You see or sense yourself being born. Continuing on the path down and around, to your earliest childhood, you see yourself taking your first steps, forming words, reaching out and grasping things, learning to feed yourself. Further down you see yourself learning to tie your own shoes and attending your first days at school. Continuing down you see yourself learning games and reaching out to other children. As you continue you see yourself growing up fast and learning many things. You see your adolescence. Farther along you observe stages of your own life until today. (Pause.)

You may feel that you have harvested the wisdom of culture and civilization and the wisdom of yourself. You continue down within the mountain. You are meeting characters from mythology and from great religious traditions: the Buddha, Krishna, Quetzalcoatl, Lao-Tse, the great gods and goddesses, the hero with a thousand faces, and yes, Moses and Abraham, Amos and Isaiah, John the Baptist, Mother Mary, Mary Magdalene, Jesus. As you continue down the mountain it seems that you have some gleanings of their wisdom.

Suddenly you find yourself at the very bottom of the inside of the mountain. There you discover a door of baked mud. Going through it, you find that it leads to a hallway and to a door of water. You pass through the door of water, and it leads to a door of fire. You pass through the door of fire, and it leads to a door of winds. You lean against the winds and pass through. This leads to a door of bronze, and you pass through. This door leads to a door of silver. You pass through the door of silver and find a door of gold.

At the door of gold there is a shining figure who says to you: "Through this door is the Sophia.

Through this door is the Wise One herself, the incarnation of Wisdom. When you pass through this door, you will be in the presence of the Sophia. There you must ask your question. You may see her or you may sense her. But know that she is there. She who is Wisdom itself." When you are in her ambiance, whether you see her or hear her or sense her or feel her, ask your question. Her answers may come in words or in images or even in feelings.

(If the visit to the Sophia is to be done as a short process the guide will say:)

You now have four minutes of clock time, equal to all the time you need, to be in the presence of the Sophia and ask your question and receive her answers. (Four minutes.)

Thanking the Sophia for her wisdom and kindness, and knowing that you can always return to visit her again, begin now to go back through the door of gold, the door of silver, of bronze, beyond the doors of winds, of fire, of water, of earth, beyond the spiral of the stages of mythical and spiritual lives, beyond the spiral of the stages of your own life, reaching the top of the mountain. Now go down the spiral path on the outside of the mountain, through the stages of culture and history. Now reach your own time in this room and this moment. Open your eyes, sit up and stretch, and, if you wish, share your experiences with someone.

(If the decision is to stay and dream together throughout the night then the guide will say:)

Now staying there in her room, you sleep and dream and dream of your question, and receive deeply from her—in this realm beyond the gold door, beyond the silver door, beyond the bronze door, be-

yond the door of winds, beyond the door of fire,
beyond the door of water, beyond the door of earth,
beyond the stages of mythical and spiritual lives, beyond the stages of your own life, beyond the stages of
culture and history and pre-history. Remain in this
place where the deepest wisdom may arise in your
dream, may arise in your insight, may arise in your
knowing. Now a voice is reading from the gnostic
gospels. You need not listen; it will enter some level
of your consciousness. You will sleep, and dream,
and remember and deepen. You will come to wisdom,
and you will remember your dream or insight.

Pass now through the golden door, as in the ancient gnostic form of Sophia. Pass through the golden
door and enter the Realm of Sophia, to sleep and
dream. May the dream of Wisdom come.

(Throughout the night, participants awaken and
share the reading from the Gnostic gospels. A gentle
but regular drumbeat can be kept going all night
long. Following the period of dreaming, or deepening, the following invocation is spoken.)

"I was sent forth from the power, and I have
come to those who reflect upon me. And I have been
found among those who seek after me. Look upon
me, you who reflect upon me, and you hearers, hear
me. You who are waiting for me, take me to yourselves." Thus spake the Sophia.

(Whenever the process is deemed ended, the
participants should share their dreams and visions,
ideas and insights. No image or idea is too trivial, no
dream fragment too banal. Discussion and even enactment of a dream may provoke other participants to
understand what a dream means in their own lives.
Thus one person's dream can be *therapeic* for all oth-

ers, and a personal understanding moves into more universal formulations.)

NOTES

1. *The Nag Hammadi Library*, edited by J. M. Robinson [New York: Harper and Row, 1977]. Hereafter cited as NHL.

2. Elaine Pagels, *The Gnostic Gospels* [New York: Random House, 1979].

3. Stephan A. Hoeller, *Jung and the Lost Gospels* [Wheaton, IL: Theosophical Publishing House, 1989].

4. *The Gospel of Philip*, 62.32-64.5, in NHL, p. 118.

5. *The Dialogue of the Savior*, 142.16-19, in NHL, p. 237.

6. *The Gospel of Thomas*, 38.4-10, in NHL, p. 121.

7. *The Gospel of Truth*, 29.8-30.12, in NHL, p. 43.

8. *The Gospel of Thomas*, 45. 30-33, in NHL, p. 126.

9. *Ibid.*, 33.11-13, in NHL, p. 118.

10. *Ibid.*, 38.23-29, in NHL, p. 121.

11. *Ibid.*, 32.14-19, in NHL, p. 118.

12. The complaints of Irenaeus against the gnostics can be found in his work *Libros Quinque Adversus Haereses*. For years this volume of brilliant and scholarly polemics served as the major source of knowledge about the gnostics.

13. *The Gospel of Thomas*, 32.19-33.5, in NHL, p. 118.

14. *Ibid.*, 42.7-51.18, in NHL, pp. 123-130 *passim.*

15. This is my translation, based upon the text described by Charles Eliot in his *Japanese Buddhism*, [New York: Barnes and Noble, 1969, pp. 109-120].

16. I am grateful to the late Winifred Babcock for introducing me to the ideas of Preston Harold concerning Christhood and identity. Harold's approach can be found in Preston Harold, *The Shining Stranger*. New York: Dodd, Mead and Company, 1967. Preston Harold and Winifred Babcock, *The Single Reality.* New York: Dodd, Mead and Company, 1971.

The Mystery of Love

Love is evolutionary energy *par excellence.* It is the force that allows us to go beyond all our conditions, our expectations, and our impediments. It carries us across the thresholds of our lives and allows us to be seized by possibility.

Whenever we look at the history and psychology of anything that really works over a long period of time—be it the miracle of birth, the miracle of friendship, the miracle of responding to creative challenge with courage and joy, or the miracle of going beyond one's boundaries—invariably we find at the source some profound kind of loving. It may be the love of an idea, or a child, or a friend, or God. It is never ineffectual or ephemeral. It is not conceptual or philosophical. It is feisty and rich, and it seizes us beyond all expectation. And we agree to be seized. One of the major problems with present Western notions of loving is that they often neglect the question of divine seizure; we have no psychology of sacred seizure.

One of the greatest privileges of my life was the opportunity of knowing a man given to divine seizure. He was so loving of everyone and everything he saw or met that the universe turned a corner for those of us fortunate enough to be in his presence. His was truly the Christic journey, and his path was strewed with many miracles of love made manifest. Let me tell you what being with him was like. Let me tell you about walking the dog with Mr. Tayer.[1]

When I was about fourteen, I used to run down Park Avenue in New York City, late for high school. I was a big overgrown girl (five feet eleven by the age of eleven). One day I literally ran into a rather frail old gentleman in his seventies and knocked the wind out of him. He laughed as I helped him to his feet and asked me in French-accented speech, "Are you planning to run like that for the rest of your life?"

"Yes, sir," I replied. "It looks that way."

"Well, bon voyage!" he said.

"Bon voyage!" I answered and sped on my way.

About a week later I was walking down Park Avenue with my fox terrier, Champ, and again I met the old gentleman.

"Ah," he greeted me, "my friend the runner, and with a fox terrier. I knew one like that many years ago in France. Where are you going?"

"Well, sir," I replied, "I'm taking Champ to Central Park."

"I will go with you," he informed me. "I will take my constitutional."

Thereafter, for about a year or so, the old gentleman and I would meet and walk together in Central Park, often several times a week. He had a long French name but asked me to call him by the first part of it, which as far as I could make out was "Mr. Tayer."

The walks were magical and full of delight. Not only did Mr. Tayer seem to have absolutely no self-consciousness, but he was always being seized by wonder and astonishment over the simplest things. He was constantly and literally falling into love. I remember one time he suddenly fell on his knees, his long Gallic nose raking the ground, and exclaimed to me, "Jeanne, look at the caterpillar. Ahhhhh!" I joined him on the ground to see what had evoked so profound a response that he was seized by the essence of caterpillar. "How beautiful it is," he remarked, "this little green being with its wonderful funny little feet. Exquisite! Little furry body, little green feet on the road to metamorphosis." He then regarded me with equal delight. "Jeanne, can you feel yourself to be a caterpillar?" "Oh yes," I replied with the baleful knowing of a gangly, pimply faced teenager. "Then think of your own metamorphosis," he suggested. "What will you be when you become a butterfly, une papillon, eh? What is the butterfly of Jeanne?" (What a great question for a fourteen-year-old girl!) His long, gothic, comic-tragic face would nod with wonder.

"Eh, Jeanne, look at the clouds! God's calligraphy in the sky! All that transforming, moving, changing, dissolving, becoming. Jeanne, become a cloud and become all the forms that ever were."

Or there was the time that Mr. Tayer and I leaned into the strong wind that suddenly whipped through Central Park, and he told me, "Jeanne, sniff the wind." I joined him in taking great snorts of wind. "The same wind may have once been sniffed by Jesus Christ (sniff), by Alexander the Great (sniff), by Napoleon (sniff), by Voltaire (sniff), by Marie Antoinette (sniff)!" (There seemed to be a lot of French people in that wind.) "Now sniff this next gust of wind in very deeply for it contains . . . JEANNE D'ARC! Sniff the wind once sniffed by Jeanne d'Arc. Be filled with the winds of history."

It was wonderful. People of all ages followed us around, laughing—not at us but with us. Old Mr. Tayer was truly diaphanous to every moment. Being with him was like being in attendance at God's own party, a continuous celebration of life and its mysteries. But mostly Mr. Tayer was so full of vital sap and juice that he seemed to flow with everything. Always he saw the interconnections between things—the way that everything in the universe, from fox terriers to tree bark to somebody's red hat to the mind of God, was related to everything else and was very, very good. He wasn't merely a great appreciator, engaged by all his senses. He was truly penetrated by the reality that was yearning for him as much as he was yearning for it. He talked to the trees, to the wind, to the rocks as dear friends, as beloved even. "Ah, my friend, the mica schist layer, do you remember when . . . ?" And I would swear that the mica schist would begin to glitter back. I mean, mica schist will do that, but on a cloudy day?! Everything was treated as personal, as sentient, as "thou." And everything that was thou was ensouled with being, and it thou-ed back to him. So when I walked with him, I felt as though a spotlight was following us, bringing radiance and light everywhere. And I was constantly seized by astonishment in the presence of this infinitely beautiful man, who radiated such sweetness, such kindness.

I remember one occasion when he was quietly watching a very old woman watching a young boy play a game. "Madame," he suddenly addressed her. She looked up, surprised that a stranger in Central Park would speak to her. "Madame," he repeated, "why are you so fascinated by what that little boy is doing?" The old woman was startled by the question, but the kindly face of Mr. Tayer seemed to allay her fears and evoke her memories. "Well sir," she replied in an ancient but pensive voice, "the game that boy is playing is like one I played in this park around 1880, only it's a mite different." We noticed that the boy was listening, so Mr. Tayer promptly included him in the conversation. "Young fellow, would you like to learn the game as it was played so many years ago?" "Well, yeah, sure, why not?" the boy replied. And soon the young boy and the old woman were making friends and sharing old and new variations on the game (as unlikely an incident to occur in Central Park as could be imagined).

Perhaps the most extraordinary thing about Mr. Tayer was the way that he would suddenly look at you. He looked at you with wonder and astonishment joined to unconditional love, joined to a whimsical regarding of you as the cluttered house that hides the holy one. I felt myself primed to the depths by such seeing. I felt evolutionary forces wake up in me by such seeing, every cell and thought and potential palpably changed. I was quickened, greened, awakened by such seeing, and the defeats and denigrations of adolescence redeemed. I would go home and tell my mother, who was a little skeptical about my walking with an old man in the park so often, "Mother, I was with my old man again, and when I am with him, I leave my littleness behind." That deeply moved her. You could not be stuck in littleness and be in the radiant field of Mr. Tayer.

The last time I ever saw him was the Thursday before Easter Sunday, 1955. I brought him the shell of a snail. "Ah, escargot," he exclaimed, and then proceeded to wax ecstatic for the better part of an hour. Snail shells, galaxies, the convolutions in the brain, the whorl of flowers and the meanderings of rivers were taken up into a great hymn to the spiralling evolution of spirit and matter. When he had finished, his voice dropped, and he whispered almost in prayer, "Omega . . . omega . . . omega. . . ." Finally he looked up and said to me quietly, "Au revoir, Jeanne."

"Au revoir, Mr. Tayer," I replied, "I'll meet you at the same time next Tuesday."

For some reason, Champ, my fox terrier, didn't want to budge. When I pulled him along, he whimpered, his tail between his legs, looking back at Mr. Tayer. The following Tuesday I was there waiting where we always met at the corner of Park Avenue and 84th Street. He didn't come. The following Thursday I waited again. Still he didn't come. The dog looked up at me sadly. For the next eight weeks I continued to wait, but he never came again. It turned out that he had suddenly died that Easter Sunday, but I didn't find that out for years.

Some years later, someone handed me a book without a cover. As I read the book I found it strangely familiar in its concepts. Occasional words and expressions loomed up as echoes from my past. When later in the book, I came across the concept of the "omega point," I was certain. I asked to see the jacket of the book, *The Phenomenon of Man*, looked at the author's picture, and, of course, recognized him immediately. There was no forgetting or mistaking that face. Mr. Tayer was Teilhard de Chardin, the great priest-scientist, poet and mystic, and during that lovely and luminous year I had been meeting him outside the Jesuit rectory of St. Ignatius, where he was living at the time.

I have often wondered if it was my simplicity and innocence that allowed the fullness of Teilhard's being to be revealed. To me he was never the great priest-paleontologist Teilhard de Chardin. He was old

Mr. Tayer. Why did he always come and walk with me every Tuesday and Thursday, even though I'm sure he had better things to do? Was it that in seeing me so completely, he himself could be completely seen at a time when his writings and his work were proscribed by the Church, when he was not permitted to teach, or even to talk about his ideas? As I later found out, at that time he was undergoing the most excruciating agony there is, the agony of utter disempowerment and psychological crucifixion. And yet to me he was always so present—whimsical, engaging, empowering. How could that be? I think it was because Teilhard had what few Church officials had— the power and grace of the Love that passes all understanding. He could write about love being the evolutionary force, the omega point, that lures the world and ourselves into becoming, because he experienced that love in a piece of rock, in the wag of a dog's tail, in the eyes of a child. He was so in love with everything that he talked in great particularity, even to me as an adolescent, about the desire that atoms have for each other, the yearning of molecules, of organisms, of bodies, of planets, of galaxies. He conveyed the longing of all creation for that radiant bonding, for joining, for the deepening of its condition, for becoming more by virtue of yearning for and finding the other. He knew about the search for the Beloved. His model was Christ. For Teilhard de Chardin, Christ was the Beloved of the soul.

As we saw in the chapter "The Mystery of Identity," Christ was the mighty quickener of the I Am as Love incarnate. And he taught that the yoke, or yoga, between the local self and the Deep Self is love. At a time in the evolution of humankind when our charge is to love or perish, the survival of our planet depends upon our allowing the transforming power of love to yoke our little, local selves to the depths of the I Am. Christ gave as the first and greatest commandment: "Thou shalt love the Lord thy God with all thy heart, and with all thy soul, and with all thy mind," thus turning the human vision inward to love and to be loved by the great Beloved within. It is this life-giving relationship with the inner Beloved that provides both form and focus to life. It is the great Yearner and the great Yearning that source transformation.

Jesus is very clear that the dynamic relationship with the Beloved is one of sustained mutuality: you cherish God as you are cherished; you hold the god-ded being within, as you are held. Because this experience of mutuality may be foreign to much of Western experience, with its emphasis on passively "resting in the arms of the Lord," the demand to be active in the relationship with the Beloved may seem impossible. But perhaps a god is a being of tremendous yearning, one who needs more love than anyone else. Maybe it is yearning that makes a god. Thus the yearning creates an emotional momentum great enough to call you to that divine-human communion wherein you as Godseed begin to bloom.

So how do you begin to engage this infinite yearning of God for you and you for God? Let us begin with the word "yearning." In Greek the term is *pothos*. It denotes an indescribable longing for something that is always seemingly over the horizon, the nostalgia for that which is often felt as infinitely wanted and infinitely unknown. In my book *The Search for the Beloved*, I describe it as the impetus for all our evolutionary striving, whose basis in the human soul is very deep. For it is the memory of a sublime union that can only be partly mirrored through human loving and partnership. It is the memory reawakened of the original union with the Beloved of the soul, the god self within, experienced as the Inner Companion, the Christ Within. In other cultures the Beloved is often clothed in the cultural archetypes of a much loved godded figure from history or mythology. Thus Buddhists often turn to the Buddha or Kwan Yin as the Beloved, Hindus develop the most exquisite emotional and spiritual relationship to Krishna or other archetypes of the divine lover, while Muslims refer to the Friend as the communicant of spiritual eros. The Hindu practice of Bhakti yoga is often an intense and highly developed form of relationship to a divine Beloved. The Beloved can also be experienced not as a cultural archetype, but as uniquely personal and original, as Beatrice was for Dante or the inner teacher Philemon was for Carl Jung. For many people today the search for the Beloved results in finding an inner reflection of God that belongs to no known historic or mythic form but whose presence is deeply felt.

However it comes about, the remembrance, discovery, and development of this friendship and communion with the Beloved is key to the work of human and planetary transformation, for it enables the emergent creative forms of the depth world, the world of your archetypal Beloved, to enter into you, and by extension to enter into space and time. Thus the critical importance of *pothos,* the yearning for the great communion that completes our reality and causes the patterns of essential and existential realms to connect.

The search for the Beloved can involve a series of practices, many of which were suggested in one form or other by the teaching and action of Jesus. For example, in evoking a sense of the Beloved, it is often important to use rich visual, auditory, tactile, olfactory and other sensory images. You try with inner imagery and active imagination to see, hear, touch the

Beloved. As we have seen, Jesus continuously did this in his rich sensory evoking of the reality of the Kingdom, the place where the Beloved dwells. Gradually, even with non-traditional figures, the Beloved will begin to take form and feeling within your inner imagery. Gradually, too, you may begin to travel to the inner Kingdom, led by the Beloved as Dante was led by Beatrice, where a kind of inner training will begin in the symbolic realms of inner space.

Another important way of evoking the Beloved is to enact the *Imago Amore,* the image of the Beloved, as if it were really present to you, and indeed within you. In the fifteenth and sixteenth centuries there were many books written under the general rubric of *The Imitation of Christ.* It was the accepted form of that period to act "as if" one were the Christed Being, thereby acquiring some of the qualities of Jesus experienced as the Beloved. And so acting "as if"you love God and are loved by God will prime the pump of your capacity for loving. The deep ontological well of loving rises when you act "as if" you are cherished by the Deeps, by God, by the Beloved in a very personal way. Remember that the Beloved is probably yearning for you as much, if not a great deal more, than you are yearning for the Beloved. Your lack of belief in this can be bridged by the "as if." Your innate dramatic character will be engaged, and before too long you will discover that you truly do love the Beloved of your soul, and, from the abundance of this loving, you discover that you also love your fellow human beings.

Contact with the Divine Beloved is never complete until some other human being feels more loved and cherished as a result of its contact. Further, as all who have ever communed with the Beloved have discovered, the more deeply you encounter the Divine

Lover, the more sensitively you feel the agony of the world; the more you are called to care more, feel more and think more deeply about decay in the social and moral order. You live in a state of radical empathy with all those in need. You are transparent to the agony of the world. Together with the Beloved, you must reach out to allay this suffering, or to do what you can in the light of the perspective of grace and the energy of spiritual partnership. One thinks of the extraordinary energy and accomplishments of Mother Teresa of Calcutta who once told me that she owed her courage and capacity to do such remarkable things to her relationship with Jesus, the Beloved of her soul. Schweitzer, Ramakrishna, and Ghandi, as well as many other transformational agents have also related the capacity for seemingly superhuman efforts and accomplishments in social transformation to communion with the Beloved.

Jesus draws attention to this in his second commandment, in which he proclaims love as the source of social transformation: "You shall love your neighbor as yourself." That is to say, profound empathy, deep cooperation, and the high ethic of love at work in human affairs will evoke the transformation of society. What Jesus is proposing is an intensive and extensive use of empathy raised to a new degree. It was the German poet Holderlin who said in *Hyperion*, "He who understands you must share your greatness and your desperation." The high art of empathic loving means sharing the desperation *and* the greatness in your neighbor's life.

In empathy you experience in yourself what is happening to another; conversely, another suffers whatever is happening to you. Empathy is not sympathy; it is a dynamic resonance, a *mysterium conjunctiones*, in which in some sense you and another incarnate each other. Because human beings are gifted with "leaky margins," we have a profound capacity to become each other. If, in some future branch of science, we are able to take pictures of what is actually going on in the subtle fields of life between people, we will probably be able to see fields of resonance around and between our bodies. And at some point there will probably be a physiology and a psychology of "leakiness."

Deep empathy, then, is not vicarious experience, for it rises from the depth world, and in its most developed form, from our relationship to the Beloved. It is, perhaps, the chief characteristic of God. Have you ever felt yourself sending or receiving empathy from someone not physically present? Don't dismiss these phenomena, for they constitute something very profound. To cherish them is to allow them to come into being, to happen for you. Only through empathy is it possible to step into another's shoes without displacing him or her, or losing one's own identity. Empathy makes this not only possible, but mandatory. When the experience of humankind has evolved to the God-quality of empathy, then what we call "sin," the abuse of another, of yourself, of nature, will no longer be possible, for the state of empathy will cause you to instinctively withdraw your mind and hand from abuse. You will know absolutely that wounding the part is wounding the whole.

Every human being has a unique destiny, an entelechy. In communion with the Beloved, you begin to have a profound respect and even awe for another person's godded potential. Certainly one of the primary exemplars of this was Jesus, who could say and do remarkable things for others and be in reverence before them. In his state of I Am-ness, which we now see was union with the Beloved, Jesus lived in the state of continuously being cherished by the Beloved, and so cherishing others. He became the medium for the magnificence of the other, the channeler and evocateur for others of their greatest creative expression. In high empathy there is always high empowerment—a quickening, an evolutionary yeasting of the other. The Christos is always the "you" who is in reverence before the Godseed in the other. In the mystery of love, as you learn to truly love another, you find the Divine Lover revealed within that other human being. That Divine Lover mirrors your Beloved and is, in some sense, the same. Then you cannot do enough for the other.

The empathic relationship to the Beloved also frees you from obsession with the past and dread of the future, for you become radically present to the present moment, but also present to the depth world of timelessness where the Beloved lives. You have a kind of temporal "double vision" which allows you to see loved ones both in the fullness of their spiritual glory and in their local caughtness. You see them, as I now understand, in the way that Teilhard saw me, with the double vision that releases and empowers the other to become who or what he or she truly is. This is the look of love. In such a meeting and acknowledgment the luminous third party, the High Being, the Spirit, the Beloved of the soul, enters as partner to the exchange. "Where two or more are gathered in My Name, there I am present," said Christ. Relationship to the Beloved calls up the Depths into full partnership, and thus transformation, be it miracles, healings, or new knowledge, can occur. Anything becomes possible, including the feeding of five thousand people.

In multiplying the loaves and fishes, Jesus evidenced the knowing that is a loving: "We will eat; I

love you; of course there is plenty." And people suddenly found that there was more food than they
could possibly eat. The miracle of the loaves and fishes partakes of the same phenomenon that Arthur C.
Clarke describes in his wonderful book *Profiles of the
Future* as the imminent technical possibility of "replication." Technologically, "replication," if it ever happens, will involve the use of an instrument that can
scan anything, say an apple, for its molecular structure, and then, out of this knowledge, create apples.
Indeed, certain states of consciousness, of which loving resonance is one, seem to heighten the very creative structure of reality, so that images of intention
attract the appropriate fields, molecules and elec-
tromagnetic forces, either to accelerate the creative
process or draw form into empty space. Love lures
the patterns of creation out of the void.

We seem to be close to the time of discovering
what has been known for millennia—that what can
be done through instrumentation can be done
through the far more complex, efficient instrument of
the body-mind-psyche. Certainly the capacity of
people in loving resonance and empathy to greatly
enhance their co-creative ventures is a phenomenon
that cannot be denied. I have seen many ventures
that were badly planned, undercapitalized and ill
thought out, but in the presence of loving resonance,
they succeeded. I have also seen complex, intricate,
organizationally developed plans, involving brilliant,
cooperative people. But where there was no love,
many of these well-capitalized ventures failed.

Plato's *Symposium* is probably the master statement of the co-creative power of people who both
love each other and are in relationship to their spiritual Beloveds. With his loving partner, Dion, Plato

created the Academy, the model for all higher education. In a state of creative, loving resonance, one experiences the lure of becoming, and from the depth
world of the Beloved come pattern, form, substance,
everything. The right person suddenly appears, the
right occasion, the right amount of support. Where
love rules, abundance is scooped from abundance,
and still more abundance remains.

Loving empathy can be intrapersonal as well as
interpersonal. You can enter into empathy with the
polyphrenic "crew" of yourself, "marrying" yourself,
as it were, on all levels. Meister Eckhart characterized
this kind of empathy as God laughing at the soul and
the soul laughing back at God.

As he was portrayed in both the orthodox and
the gnostic canon, Jesus was always in love, always
in empathy. He was in empathy with nature; all living things were precious and delightful to him—
sparrows, lilies, children. He sought the open beauty
of mountains and sea, the solitude of deserts. He also
went to cities, marketplaces, parties, feasts, and to
the temple. He loved to eat and drink. His imagery
was full of sensory splendor. He delighted in the
abundant life and aided the poor, but he did not extol
poverty. He respected the Sabbath, but said, "The
Sabbath is made for man, not man for the Sabbath."
He despised exhibitions of piety, vain repetitions,
brutality, and self-debasement. His was a total and
continuous loving. Of course he could evoke the right
event at the right moment because he was constantly
falling in love. He stood in awe and astonishment
before the other, possessed with a sense of wonder in
the presence of all things.

Now you will enter the transformative realm of
empathetic love through a group process.

Process—The Enactment
of the Images of Love

TIME—Approximately sixty minutes

MUSIC—Gregorian chants; Samuel Barber's "Adagio for Strings"; Marais' "La Sonnerie de Sainte Genevieve"; Pachelbel's "Canon in D Minor."

MATERIALS—Enough fragrant oils for the whole group.

THE PROCESS—The reader or guide will say:

Wander around the group until you find a partner, preferably someone you do not know very well—although there is no prohibition against partnering with someone you do know well if that feels appropriate. We are going to actually enact some of the iconic images of love from the New Testament—images that have emerged from Jesus' story of love and relationship. And when you have discovered the partner appropriate to you, sit down together. As we play a Gregorian chant, turn to your partner and share with him or her what most fills your heart with wonder. What it is that astonishes you, that evokes awe and wonder? Then the other partner shares what fills him or her with awe and wonder. (Allow five minutes for each partner.)

Now sitting opposite one another, gently clasp hands with your partner and close your eyes. Begin to breathe together. Begin by breathing quietly, feeling the life force flowing back and forth from your hands to your partner's hands and your partner's hands to you. (Three minutes.)

And now feel yourself in a field of wonder, filled and pervaded by the field of wonder that has existed since time began. In this field of wonder, open your eyes and gently speak back and forth, without conditions, without determining ahead of time what you are going to say. Speak your sense of wonder before the fullness of being of the other, your partner. Beginning now, just let it flow out, knowing that it goes beyond your own personal or historical knowing. It is the God-Self in you seeing the God-Self in the other. (Five minutes)

Now let us begin with some of the icons, the images from the life of Christ. Don't speak now. Merely enact the icons and let the fullness of the power of the images fill you with loving resonance. First, one of you will be Jesus and the other John, the Beloved Disciple, who rests his head on the shoulder of Jesus. Just enact this icon without commentary, letting the field of richness that surrounds this image astonish you, as it has astonished so many for thousands of years. Just rest your head on Jesus' shoulder. It is just a simple act. (Now Barber's "Adagio for Strings" will be played.) (Three minutes)

Now change roles: the one who was Jesus becomes John and vice versa, so that each partner experiences the icon from a different perspective. Allow the warmth of millennia to flow between the two of you. (Three minutes)

Now recall the image of Mary Magdalene washing and massaging the feet of Jesus with infinite love. Perform this act of infinite love. One of you will be Jesus and the other Mary Magdalene. The one who is enacting Mary massages Jesus' feet with fine oils, great tenderness, and a sense of deep communion.

The one who is the Christos receives that loving, receives it with deep, loving response. (Five minutes)

Now change roles: Let Jesus be Mary Magdalene and Mary be the Christos. With great loving communion wash and massage the feet. (Five minutes)

Now one of you become the image of the loving Madonna, holding the Infant, the infinite Infant, deeply cherishing the Holy Child in wonder and astonishment. As the Holy Child, know yourself deeply cherished and loved by the Madonna. (Three minutes)

Again change roles. Let the child become the Madonna, holding the other as the Holy Child with such sweetness, knowing the loving joy of deep communion. (Three minutes)

Now the baby stretches out its body, growing, growing. And the child becomes the Beloved Son, lying dead in the lap of the grieving Mary, the mourning Mary, the Mater Dolorosa, the Mother of Sorrows. The grown-up child lies dead on Mary's lap, and Mary feels so much love and grief, mourning as the Beloved Son lies on her lap. (Three minutes)

Changing roles, again assume the position of the Pieta, the grieving Mary and the dead Jesus. (Three minutes)

Now both partners stand and face each other. Place your hands on the other's shoulders. This time become the Resurrected Ones, renewed in the fullness of your being, having returned from the dead places in your life. Each of you is the Resurrected Christos. Without speaking, face your partner so you can see him or her deeply. As the music plays, look at each other in wonder and astonishment and in the fullness of love. (Marais' "La Sonnerie de Sainte Gen-evieve" is played.) (Seven minutes)

Now speak back and forth of what you have known, what you have seen, what you have discovered in the enactment of the icons. (Pachelbel's "Canon in D Minor" is played.)

Now just hold each other, you and your partner. Also let yourself be held by the I Am, by God, by the Beloved of the Soul. Feel yourself cherished by the Beloved who yearns for you as much, if not more, than you yearn for the Beloved. Feel yourself as the Two in One. And when the Two become the One and the One becomes the Many and the Many become God and the Male becomes Female and the Female becomes Male, then the Kingdom is here.

Swaying gently back and forth, be cherished, be loved by whatever it is that you know as the spiritual Beloved. For you have seen so much wonder and astonishment in each other. Feel the yearning and the cherishing of God for you, both individually and together. Know yourself cherished. The Third Party is present. The Beloved is here.

Now together dance with God. The two of you together dance the Beloved reflected in each other. Dance the great loving. You are the Dance, for there is only the Dance. (The word "Alleluia" is sung to Pachelbel's "Canon in D Minor" to close the process.)

NOTES

1. I tell a condensed version of this story in my book *Life Force*, [New York: Delta, 1980], pp. 218-220.

The Mystery of Miracles

Miracles are the conscious activation of more patterns of reality than are usually seen in local, limited, unloving consciousness. In a state of love, in a state of resonance, in a state of I Am-ness, you experience the thinning of the membranes between the worlds. And when the membranes are thinned, all kinds of new realities present themselves to be orchestrated. It is then, of course, that you can perform miracles. In many parts of the Eastern world, miraculous powers are known as *siddhis* and are described in the Yoga Sutras of Patanjali as including knowledge of past and future, telepathy, invisibility, and levitation. These events are very dramatic when they occur, but they do very little to change human nature, and tend to fill the inexperienced practitioner with illusions of his or her own enlightenment. Thus, many Eastern teachers advise against paying attention to miracles.

Today, however, we need to look at the nature of *siddhis* and miracles in a much more creative and productive way, especially when the nature of reality is being stretched by the sheer intensity of our times. If we don't perform miracles, what will happen? Entropy patterns will speed up, and we will have a very long sunset effect. Miracles are the telling proof that what we call "ordinary reality" (and its workings) is only one special case in the nature of reality itself. There are multiple laws of form, and just as different states of consciousness give us access to different capacities, so different states of planetary awareness give us new options and opportunities—to partner the planet, for example, and to take responsibility for biological and evolutionary governance, which, in our ancestors' terms, would be an incredible miracle.

The local law of form always contains within itself the seeds of its own transcendence. In David Bohm's theory, the primary implicate order of reality contains the enfolded patterns behind all possible realities, including the many alternative ways of working in the world. Our problem is that we have been conditioned in the mind-set of a particular explicate reality to give belief only to the local law of form.

We are the gods that our ancestors spoke of. We can move mountains in seconds. We can communicate instantaneously with any part of the globe. Every night we look at our luminous picture boxes to find out what the other gods are up to. But we are still archaic in terms of mythic structures. We still suffer from the disabilities of the archaic gods. And that is why the gods have to be grown. Thus the doing of miracles is not simply a question of doing remarkable things. Rather, your godding self, which performs the miracles, has to be regrown and extended. We are the ones who deepen the archetypal, mythic realm, which waits at the crossroads, yearning to be released, to be extended. We are at a time, as Kazantzakis has said, of the saving of the gods, the regrowing of the gods. We are at a time when the local law of form has become too limited a paradigm and we know there is a much larger form waiting to be revealed.

Once, while traveling among aboriginal cultures, I told my host that I had to get a message to the airport many miles away to charter a small plane. There were no phones, no radios and no other way of sending a message such a long distance. "Oh, we'll take care of that," he assured me. "But you don't have a telephone," I said. "That's all right," he said, and proceeded to go up to a certain tree to which he relayed my message. "Don't worry, the plane will be there," he told me, grinning happily. When I finally arrived at the small airport, indeed the plane was there. "What happened?" I asked the pilot. "Oh, we got the tree message," he said.

Now to our local law of form, such an incident is patently absurd, and it is easy to believe that I must have been duped. However, anthropologists are filled with stories (which they are careful not to publish in scholarly journals) about alternative laws of living and working in the world. Having finished largely with drawing maps of the geophysical world, we may soon have both the courage and the motivation to create cartographies of alternative laws of nature. What had previously been perceived as extraordinary may now be seen as an interesting variation of the ordinary.

I have always found that an exploration of the nature of the creative process helps to illuminate the nature of miracles. For creative thought is also the conscious awareness and activation of more and more patterns of reality. It involves tapping into the loaded codices of implicate reality for other patterns of possible expression. In this sense the creative person always performs miracles.

In my close friendship with and study of Margaret Mead, I observed this phenomenon of the "miraculous" element that was consonant with her high creativity. She was always aware of many different patterns of reality, not just from her anthropological training, but also because her nature would not permit her closing her accounts with reality. "I am perfectly prepared to believe that there are three thousand separate realities going on in this room right now," she would say. The pattern of fortunate coincidence around her was astonishing. Synchronicities just seemed to flourish in her presence: the right person, the right book, the right slip of the tongue that provided valuable associations, being in the right place at the right time to receive the next step in a project or an idea. The stuff of miracles was the stuff of Margaret's life. I would see these things and say, "Margaret, you are blessed." And she would say, "Yes, I am blessed. That is the condition of my life. I am blessed." On those very rare occasions when things did not work out, she would scream and yell at the universe, and then it was as if the universe said, "Yes, Margaret," and things would fall back into their usual blessed state again.

In my book *The Possible Human*, I described studies made of deep meditators and of people in high creative states. The research seemed to show that on a physiological level there occurs an extraordinary degree of resonance: a resonance in terms of the brain in macrophasic wave function (different brain waves singing the same song, as it were). A resonance also occurs with the cross exchange of different neurological systems, which in turn drives the organism to systemic transformation and a new level of awareness and use of its own capacity. Then the brain/mind system seems able to select out of the depth realities, with which it is now more deeply connected, other laws or expressions that allow for miracles, creativity, and even transformation (a form of resurrection).

In high creative thought these pan-systemic changes in the organism are perhaps reflected in the coming of an almost unimpeded flow of ideas, information, memories and patterns that tend to move in organic groupings. These patterns themselves are desirous of expression and set up what we could call an organic phase-coherence with the surrounding fields of reality. Thus the very building matrices of reality— that is, the appropriate people, ideas, books, associations, opportunities—begin to organize around the creative intention.[1]

Like sunlight and the nutrients of earth and air organizing around the new buds of springtime, budding intentions organize in resonance with depth or holonomic reality, evoking from this primary order the proper nutrients for the emergence of the physical expression of the creative intention—be it a novel, a symphony, a dissertation, a new project, a relationship, a business, a community enterprise, or a quality of life. In this process you discover that you are no longer boxed in by your local personality; rather, it becomes that through which the creative and evolutionary patterns of the archetypal and the Deep Self realms of being enter into space and time. Herein one does the work of the gods; that is why the creative act is also the godly act. It is also why research shows that mystical or religious experience almost always yields an increase in creative work, while creative endeavors yield unitive and transformative experiences. The physics and the metaphysics of the miraculous, the mystical, and the high creative experience seem to be very similar, if not the same.

When creativity is further engaged by the factor

of faith, then the previously unimagined becomes possible. Jesus said that if we but had the faith of a grain of mustard seed, we could move mountains. Have you ever planted a mustard seed? If ever you do, you will be most surprised at the large, glorious bush that emerges, so abundant that birds will build their nests and raise their young in its branches. Faith takes the mustard seed of ourselves, replants it in the soil of possibility, allows for the nutrients of the many levels of reality to feed us, and nourishes the new plant in us. Faith weaves new dendritic connections in the brain, strengthens the neuronal networks, enhances and gives flexibility and color to our motor and sensory capacities, raises our frequency and capacity of thought, evolves the self and finally, I believe, grows God in us.

Love is that which gives life to this process; love itself is increased by its own endeavor. Unbelief is suspended, for love and the resonance which it creates become quite literally all. You cannot be in a state of empathy and loving resonance with another while you are open to unbelief.

Let's look at the ways Jesus used faith, love, resonance, and the power of the I Am to accomplish miracles. Jesus named some very specific conditions that are prerequisites to the occurrence of miracles. He said, "If ye have faith and doubt not. . ." That is, a faith so assured and focused that the nagging doubts of disbelief are suspended and your whole person is in synchrony with the creative realm of possibility. "All things whatsoever ye ask in prayer, believing, ye shall receive." Prayer is a going beneath or beyond the surface crust of consciousness to a level where the usual hedgings and conditions no longer apply. Prayer gives you access to depth levels of consciousness where depth possibilities abound.

"If ye ask anything in my name, I will do it." "My name" is I Am, and I Am is always a state of fulfillment. The beginning, the middle and the end are always implicit and existent in the I Am. Mozart, for example, dwelt in the I Am-ness of music, so that he composed by playing what he heard. Often he had the experience that the music had already been created at some deep level of his psyche and he merely wrote it down. He is reported to have said, "Where it comes from I do not know, but I thank God that it is at least Mozartish." Beethoven had the same experience; so did Wagner, as did countless other creative artists and scientists. In high creativity the fullness of the totality is often revealed in one great fell happening, almost as an autonomous self-creating work of art.

Another condition Jesus specified was: "If two of you shall agree on earth as touching anything that they shall ask, it shall be done for them of my Father which is in heaven." That is, if two of you are in loving resonance, then you are amplified, you are extended throughout earth and heaven, and your mutual creative intention is assured. You then become co-creators with God of the things that need to enter time.

Jesus seemed to regard despair as the quality of mind that impedes the flow of the miraculous. Despair is more often than not the source of our sickness, and release from despair is the source of our healing. Kierkegaard said that despair is never ultimately over any external object, but always over ourselves. It keeps us in fear and trembling and leads us toward death. About thirty years ago there was a telling study made in a Swiss hospital that shed light on the subject of despair. The emotional situation surrounding the life of each of the forty-two patients in the hospital was investigated. The study revealed that all but one had suffered significant despair during the year prior to hospitalization and thirty-one had undergone an experience of despair only a week prior to becoming sick and being hospitalized.

Jesus released despair while he healed. "Your sins are forgiven," he would say with enormous love and empathy. The term "sins" is an ambiguous one, for in Aramaic it also refers to the lifting of the accumulations of your life. Jesus was essentially saying, "You now have freedom from load, freedom from accumulations."

After releasing despair, Jesus would often say, "Arise and walk," or an appropriate equivalent. Now for the most part our auto-pharmacological responses indicate that we human beings have tremendous potential to deal with most of life's stresses and that nature has provided many built-in defenses that make for extraordinary protection. This curative force innate in all of us can be released in certain states of consciousness, especially when the log jam of the despairing psyche is also released. Jesus said over and over that it is not that which comes from without that makes us unclean, but that which comes from within. What happens in miracles is a healing of the internal defilement; a shock is given to the old habit response patterns.

As I have studied the nature of the miracles that Jesus performed, I have observed a remarkable phenomenology in the nature and practice of this healing. First, he rapidly induced a surprised or altered state of consciousness. Second, he informed the sick person of his or her release from psychological defilement, what we would call "old tapes." Third, he usually uttered an authoritative word or command that produced a shock. Fourth, he frequently touched the sick one in order to reinforce and direct his verbal command. What Jesus experienced internally as he performed these acts I can only surmise, but, in the light of the issues we have been exploring, I will dare to dance with angels and offer several ideas.

I believe that while Jesus was engaged in these four stages of the healing process, he was also experiencing a shift from local consciousness to I Am consciousness. Thus he could see the one to be healed from a state of empathy and loving resonance; the sick one was, in effect, placed in the I Am reality, wherein he or she was perfect.

Next, Jesus directed chi energy, or heightened field energy, and amplified the fields within and about the person, activating much more of the brain-mind-psyche and allowing the power of the Depths, the great original Patterns that are the Patterns of Re-creation, to rise. Thus the channels through which the deeper healing and wholing patterns can emerge were strengthened. In love and empathy, Jesus was fielding the other.

In a number of miracles Jesus performed, the patient or recipient was not even physically present: the centurion's servant, the woman whose daughter was sick, and the man who pleads for his son. In these cases healing power was sent through waves of resonance and empathy or as an intensive image to the surrogate for the healing—to the centurion, or to the father or mother of the sick one. In the case of the Roman centurion, his empathy and faith were so deep that he said: "Lord, I am not worthy that thou shoulds't come under my roof: but speak the word only, and my servant shall be healed." The centurion recognized the depth of Jesus' authority and power, and in response, Jesus marveled at the man's faith, unsurpassed in his experience. "And Jesus said unto the centurion, 'Go thy way; and as thou hast believed, so be it done unto thee.' And his servant was healed in the self-same hour." (Matthew 8:8-10, 13)

Without authority Jesus could accomplish little. The scriptures are explicit about this fact, for they tell us that Jesus failed to work many miracles in his home town, where he was regarded as the local boy without prestige, a common experience.

Most important of all, however, was the fact that Jesus was in love with the Depths, the dimensionality and the promise of the other. If we choose to live our lives at the level Christ lived his, we, too, must stand in a state of wonder and astonishment before the other, resonant to the infinite I Am-ness that is the ground of the other's being.

Process—The High Practice of Healing and Wholing

TIME—Approximately thirty to forty-five minutes

MUSIC—Deuter's "Ecstasy" or some sacred or inspirational music of your choice.

THE PROCESS—The reader or guide will say:

This is a High Practice for working with others, not just for healing, but also for wholing. We will make a correspondence between the internal behavior for healing and wholing and its external expression. To do this well is an art, not a science. It is one of the High Arts of human endeavor.

We will take the forms of this practice literally as we work with each other following the pattern of Jesus. You will be given directions, but you will undoubtedly find in, with and for yourself an enormous amount of variation. This is not only permitted, but demanded, because you are uniquely who you are. The form given here requires you to discover your own variations in the days and weeks to come.

With these comments as background, we are about to perform miracles. Now find a partner and twosomes spread around the room.

Decide who will be the healer-wholer and who will be the person to be healed and wholed. You will change places later. Decide now who will be the first healer and who will first be healed and wholed.

Now take each other's hands. Sit together quietly in resonance, gently feeling your life force moving in and through you both.

Just sit in resonance and breathe together. Think nothing, but feel a sort of benign sense about both yourself and the other. No big thoughts. Just a sort of easy flowing together in resonance.

Healer, now move yourself into the place of I Am. No matter how many problems you may have or how much despair you may have been feeling locally, make that shift now. This is sacred time and space, and know, Healer, that you are now moving into sacred time and space where you transcend all despair. Move into the place of the I Am.

As the Healer shifts into I Am consciousness, the partner who needs healing or wholing begins to speak about what needs healing or wholing, be it of mind, body or spirit. Healer, stay in the I Am consciousness while your partner speaks about his or her needs for healing or wholing. Begin now.

You who are about to be healed or wholed, thank the healer ahead of time for what is about to take place. Thank him or her for the healing and wholing that you are about to receive.

Now both of you look directly at each other. Healer, you who have shifted into I Am consciousness, you are the Godded Being. Look at your partner with much love and empathy. This is the first step, the induction of a communion or an altered state of consciousness. Eye-to-eye, look at your partner with God-love, with so much love and empathy that a shift in consciousness is evoked.

The next step is the command that produces a shock great enough to effect release from psychological defilements and old tapes. So, Healer, in love and empathy, say to your partner: "Your old patterns are released. Your despair is no longer necessary." Let the words come from your heart. Know it and say it and see your partner as pure and whole. Perhaps even say, "I see you pure and whole." In love and empathy say, "Your old patterns are released. I see you pure and whole." and really mean it.

As you are doing this, reach out and touch your partner. Feel your hands filled with sun, filled with love, filled with chi, the vital reorganizing energy. Pass your hands over your partner, touching the field around him or her. Feel yourself filling your partner's field with light, with the powers and patterns for the body and the mind and the soul to be re-orchestrated, your field charging your partner's field. Know yourself, Healer, to be strengthened by the I Am-ness that is using your hands as the vehicle for sending high re-creative energy. "I see you pure and whole. Your old patterns are released. Your despair is no longer necessary."

As you do this, see the other form a state of empathy as healed and in union with the One. You, the Healer, are in Union, and your I Am is speaking to your partner's I Am as the immense capacity for being healed and wholed is being activated by you.

You who are receiving, know yourself being

healed and wholed. You who are doing the healing and wholing, know your partner as being healed and whole. Absolutely.

Then sit back and, again in union, with your eyes allow the healing and the wholing pattern to emerge. You who have received, feel that new pattern emerging, feel yourself being healed and wholed. You who are Christos, I Am, know it absolutely to be happening. Sit in union of I Am with I Am in quiet.

Now from I Am to I Am, speak to each other about what you have felt and known and are. Give thanks for the Gracing that has occurred. Speak to each other about what you have felt and known and are. And give thanks for the Gracing that has occurred.

Get up now and do some stretching, staying with each other and moving a little before changing places.

Sit down again with the same partner. Take each other's hands and sit quietly in resonance with each other. The person who has been the healed now becomes the Healer and shifts from local consciousness into I Am consciousness. You who were Healer now become the one to be healed and wholed.

The new healer shifts into God consciousness, into I Am consciousness. As your partner is shifting into I Am consciousness, you who are to receive speak what it is in mind or body or spirit that needs healing or wholing.

Thank the Healer ahead of time for what is about to take place. Thank him or her for the healing and wholing that you are about to receive.

Now come to quiet. Open your eyes and look at each other. In this state of loving resonance, you who have now shifted into I Am, you who are Healer, look into the eyes of the other from the Beingness of I Am. And you who are receiving, allow your consciousness to shift or be deepened by virtue of being looked at by the extraordinary lovingness of the I Am, of the God-Self. You who are in I Am, send enormous love and empathy. You who are there to receive, receive this deeply.

At the same time, Healer, speak to your partner, releasing him or her from inner defilements, old sins, old habits, old tapes. Seeing your partner released, say, "I see you pure and whole. I know you released." Know this absolutely. Speak with great authority and confidence from your knowing. As you speak reach out and touch your partner.

Then, reaching out to the body of your partner, fill your hands with sun, with godly energy, with the chi, the vital reorganizing energy that moves the worlds apart. Pass your hands over your partner, touching the field around him or her. Send a new pattern through that field as you continue speaking with authority of release, of a new resonance, a new possibility for healing and wholing. Caress and touch the field surrounding your partner. As you do this, know yourself to be strengthened by the I Am-ness that is using your hands as the vehicle for sending high energy.

As you do this, see the other from a state of empathy as healed and in union with the One. Find yourself in Union, your I Am speaking to your partner's I Am, as the immense capacity for being healed and wholed is activated. From the authority of the I Am, field, heal, whole the other.

You who are receiving, know this deeper pattern emerging, acting in your cells and in your psyche, releasing despair, bringing the light into every part of you. Receive and be in union with the sending, I Am to I Am. Let your eyes be open as you receive deeply. "Lord, let me be an instrument of thy will."

And now from I Am to I Am, speak to each other about what you have felt and known and are. Share what has happened, what is happening. Give thanks for the Gracing that has occurred. Speak about what you are feeling and knowing and are, the healing, the wholing that you are aware of. Share what is happening and give thanks for the Gracing that has occurred. Sit where you are, not changing your position very much at this time.

(Allow approximately ten minutes for sharing.)

Now, chances are that each of you has a friend or relative who is in need of healing or wholing. If it is appropriate, tell your partner about that friend or relative. Speak succinctly about someone in need of healing or wholing who is in your thoughts right now. You are going to send healing to your partner's friend, and your partner is going to send healing to your friend. At some deep level you are going to receive the channeling for the healing being sent, and your partner will receive the channeling for the healing you are sending.

Now both of you coming to quiet, sit in I Amness. Send healing to your friend's friend. And receive the healing that is being sent from your partner to your friend. While your eyes are open and your hands are touching your partner's, send healing to the person you have just heard about, and at the same time be the channel for receiving the healing. (Approximately five minutes.)

Thank each other for serving as a channel for the healing and wholing of your friend.

NOTES

1. I discuss this in *The Possible Human,* pp. 194-200.

The Mystery of Resurrection

In the story of Jesus the resurrection is the essential miracle, the deepest mystery, and the greatest stumbling block.

The miracle of the godded one who dies or is killed and comes back to life has a long and extraordinary history in the myths and ritual patterns of many cultures, most familiarly those of ancient Greece and the ancient Near East. Isis searches for the scattered parts of her husband, Osiris, binds them together and animates him to produce new life; Demeter calls forth her daughter, Persephone, from her dwelling place in the kingdom of the Dead; Tammuz, Adonis, Dionysius all are destroyed and all are remade.

In the Greco-Roman world these acts of resurrection were celebrated in the Mystery Religions. These ecstatic forms of piety involved dramatic, highly ritualized inward journeys of anguish, grief, loss, resurrection, redemption, joy and ecstasy. The Mystery Religions provided alienated individuals lost in the nameless masses of the Roman Empire with an intimate environment and community of the saved, in which they counted as real persons and found a deeper identity. Identifying with the God-man or the Goddess-woman of the mystery cult, the initiate died to the old self and was resurrected to personal transfiguration and eternal life.

We know that in Egypt, Chaldea, Greece and India the mysteries sometimes involved initiation rites in which sufficiently trained neophytes were put into a three day death-like sleep by a hierophant or priest. In the esoteric schools it was thought that in these states the subtle body received the training it needed to impress upon the physical body a new order of being. This process involved the temporary surrender of the life spirit. There are even those who believe that Lazarus was in a state of death-like sleep when Christ called him forth.

The resurrection story of Jesus differs radically from that of the traditional mystery cult figures. By being historical, by living a human existence in space and time, Jesus brought a new dimension, that of human experience, to the transpersonal and archetypal dimension of God-Identity.

I believe that if the resurrection occurred, it was because the cosmic principle was so deeply interwoven in his human structure that it did not depart with his cold flesh on the cold stone. Indeed, the power of this principle was so strong that it re-ordered that cold flesh to warm life, and brought into the world a spirit of renewal that had never been known before.

How was this accomplished? And who accomplished it? God, or the Holy Spirit, or Jesus himself? No one can ever know. Mystics and contemplatives offer a perspective on the resurrection that seems to me to mirror their own experiences of illumination and unity. They tell us that perhaps Jesus effected his own regeneration through a profound state of self-reflection, possible only to those who have become transparent to transcendence and are coded by that experience with a quality of eternity that does not, cannot, die with death. This implies that a new order has been created within spirit, within nature, within the soul, within the meaning and matter of history. Here we move out beyond miracle into the heart of mystery, and consciousness grows into the capacity for co-creation with God. The world turns a corner, and true partnership between divine and human realms becomes possible.

Great athletes of the spirit, whose powers of inward-turning have brought them to the God-reflecting waters of the inmost soul, believe that the moments of resurrection that took place in that tomb create a kind of metaphysical jumping-off place, a fall into mystery where psychological and even theological realities end and sacramental reality begins. Here Jesus becomes Christos, ritual comes alive, all matter is shown to be holy, and the human becomes Love.

For those who are not mystics or deeply believing Christians, the story of the resurrection nevertheless holds a potency and sense of miracle that need not be lost in arguments about whether it actually happened. What is real and true about the story, for believers and non-believers alike, is that each of us has within us the capacity to bring about many varieties of resurrection. This is a mystery with many phases, one of which has to do with our capacity to be dramatically and psychophysically renewed to such an extent that we undergo a virtual death and resurrection. Anyone who has been powerfully renewed knows that he or she can speak of having been dead and then brought back to life.

Often when the body-brain-mind-psyche system

has been given a profound stimulus or shock, it becomes capable of releasing many of its old patterns and allowing itself to be pulsed to a different frequency, allowing the emergence of a different human being. The history of religious experience is full of cases of people who were changed so dramatically, sometimes in the twinkling of an eye, that the before hardly resembles the after. These people do not lose their previous knowledge, contacts or friendships, but they are released to such an amplitude of being that the before self seems Neanderthal compared to the after self, which is proto-angelic.

This rearrangement of self is not unlike what is described in Prigogine's theorem of how things grow and change in a state of creative instability. As systems become vulnerable to new information it is dispersed throughout the system, driving the system to a new regime, bringing even more vulnerability and availability to more information. More changes begin to occur systemically, more patterns and forms emerge; finally a whole new being emerges. Resurrection!

Another phase of resurrection is essentially a re-membrance, a re-membraning, of our own true nature; it is a waking up to this re-membrance. When we truly hear the message of resurrection, our latent informational systems are unlocked, our deep evolutionary coding is evoked, and more of our internal systems are recruited for whole-system transformation. We then experience a change that accelerates exponentially to such a degree that we are not the same body-brain-psyche any more. In this form of resurrection latent evolutionary systems are quickened and awakened to full manifestation.

At present there is a critical mass of new information at the same time as the releasing of tribal, insular, and national bondage. These occur along with the current density of cross-cultural and cross-information exchange. All this provides the wherewithal for the release, on a global scale, of a phenomenon that could also be described as planetary resurrection. As noted, resurrection is about being pulsed into new patterns appropriate to our new time and place. It is also about living on a continuum with extended and "resurrected" realities, be those realities Buddhas, gods, Christs, archetypes, or even the stars themselves.

Finally, the resurrection is about falling beyond the controls, habits and conditioned mind-sets of person and society in order to become transparent to transcendence. Resurrection is to engage at the core the Heart of existence and the Love that knows no limits. It is to allow for the Glory of Love to have its way with us, to encounter and surrender to That which is forever seeking us, and from this to conceive the Godseed. Resurrection presumes a void that precedes it, an emptying of our existence. Being empty, we then can be filled; being unknowing, we become knowledge; being nowhere we are suddenly a citizen in the great Kingdom.

The need for resurrection has increased in intensity in our time. We are living at the very edge of history, at a time when the whole planet is heading toward a global passion play, a planetary crucifixion. Great yellow clouds of pollution hover over major cities. The land is raped, the forests decimated. In the twenty or so years that I have been working around the globe, I have seen the increasing desertification of the world. We are truly experiencing a worldwide Golgotha.

When I travel through America, I am appalled by the limbo of shopping malls, the limbo of automobile culture, the limbo of corporate culture, the limbo of wasteland ecology, the limbo of meaninglessness, of lack of caring. Robert Coles notes the brutal competition among students in our schools that mitigates against human values. This danger is particularly apparent in the caring professions like medicine, where the competition is so fierce that often those who would make the finest healers of body and mind are strained out in favor of those whose ability to pass tests wins the approbation of the computer.

Then there is the personal limbo of our time. Many people, bereft of meaning and no longer committed to the standard brand culture, philosophy or religion of our era, have long periods in which they quite literally feel dead. Many of us feel caught up in limbos of our own and others' making. We long for the call to arise. We long for resurrection, and we refuse to believe the signs that it may already be in our midst. Resurrected ones are walking among us, and we mistake them, as did the three women at the resurrection of Christ, for pleasant hippie-type gardeners. Perhaps in our time the longing itself becomes the experience. Perhaps we can paraphrase Meister Eckhart when he said, "The eye by which I see God is the same eye by which God sees me." Now we can say that the longing with which we yearn for God is the same longing with which God yearns for us. I believe that the strength of that mutual longing can give us the evolutionary passion to roll away the stone, the stumbling blocks that keep us sealed away and dead to the renewal of life.

THE WALK TO EMMAUS

The mystery of the journey of Jesus in the world does not end with the resurrection but with another journey, a walk on the road to Emmaus. As the gospel of

Luke recounts, several days after the crucifixion, two men were walking along the road to Emmaus, a town some seven miles from Jerusalem. They were deeply absorbed in their conversation and hardly noticed when a third man quietly joined them on the road. After a while this stranger interrupted to ask what they were talking about so intently and with such sadness. They told him that they were discussing the condemnation and death of Jesus and the discovery of the empty tomb by certain women of their company who had come back saying that they had even seen a vision of angels, who said that Jesus was alive. The stranger agreed that Jesus was indeed living, and as they continued to walk together took them through an interpretation of the scriptures, showing them in chapter and verse how everything that had happened had in fact been foretold.

The two men felt great warmth in their hearts toward the stranger, and when they reached the house in Emmaus where they would be staying, they invited him to join them as it was now late. The stranger agreed and went to dinner with them, blessing the bread and breaking it to give to them. At that moment they underwent a shock of recognition and knew the man not as stranger, but as Jesus. Immediately he disappeared. The two men instantly got up and sped along the road back to Jerusalem, where they told the disciples the wonderful things that had just happened. As they were telling these things, Jesus suddenly appeared among them, quieted their fears that he was just a spirit, and invited them to handle his very physical hands and feet. Then he asked for something to eat and proceeded to chew and swallow some broiled fish. He concluded his visit by blessing and empowering them, and they were filled with great joy.

The Emmaus journey continues the mystery rites

of the resurrection in new and remarkable ways. Luke's gospel narrative is one of completion and fulfillment. Emmaus is cited as "seven miles from Jerusalem." In the tradition of sacred numbers, seven completes the quest. The Emmaus walk marks Christ's return from the eternal to the temporal world in an act of compassion, relatedness, community and, most important, concreteness. But the real presence was difficult for the disciples. "Something kept them from seeing who it was" until the moment he broke the bread and offered it to them. "Then their eyes were opened, and they recognized him."

Here we discover the Eucharist as continuing the central mystery of the Christian tradition, which ironically, and almost comically, turns out to glorify the most physical and concrete of all experiences. The ritual gesture of Jesus consecrating the bread is an enfleshment, a palpable statement of the concreteness of God-in-the-world, an earthy presence of Christ among the community of the faith.

Faith consciousness recognizes in the symbols not merely a meaning, a memory or an understanding of Christ, but a reality of the Divine in all that is human, that is ordinary, that is natural. Bread is broken together and fish is chewed. Hands and feet are extended to be touched. There is nothing abstract here, nothing of the ephemeral spook or the smoky apparition. No one is hallucinating; on the contrary, they are invited to engage together in the most sensory of communions. "Why are you troubled, and why do questionings arise in your hearts? See my hands and feet, that it is I myself. Touch me and see, for a spirit has not flesh and bones as you see that I have."

In the hidden divinity of Christ, in the substance of things unknown, in the ultimate mystery of a reality beyond our control or our images—the Godseed comes and says, "Touch me," and we are Godded and transformed in the Love of the Beloved. We can refuse to see with our eyes and hear with our ears and know with our minds. But it is difficult to doubt the reality of flesh touching flesh, and it is well nigh impossible to reject the even greater impression of heart touching heart. At this point we discover that we know nothing, but we feel everything. Surrendering to feeling, we find that being so loved we have no choice but to become love, to become the stranger on the road of everyone's Emmaus, the one who discloses the goddedness within, the one who says, "Touch me."

In this mystery and this consciousness we are required to die to our learned habits and ways of knowing, and to be reborn in a learned ignorance that is the essence of wisdom.

It was in the evening of the journey to Emmaus that this sacramental consciousness was reached, not in the fullness of the day. Thus in the darkness there is light, in the unseeing there is seeing, in the absence of Jesus there is the Christ present. Augustine once experienced a series of visions of Christ that finally began to wane. Filled with anguish at the loss of the Beloved, the saint cried out to Christ to return. Out of the darkness he heard the words, "I have disappeared right before your eyes in order for you to return into your heart to find me." Thus for the disciples of Emmaus and for Augustine the sacramental Christ did not come to liberate first their outer worlds—their Israel—from the outside in. He came to liberate them from the inside out—from that deepest place within that seemed unreachable, from that Kingdom within that seemed elusive, from that voice within that seemed silent, from that spirit within that seemed dead. For it is in the heart that the Mystery of the Eucharist transforms our lives alchemically. In our hearts, in our feelings, in the places where we are touched, the miracle of transubstantiation occurs, and spirit and matter become each other.

Thus in the resurrection of the eating, drinking, loving, empowering, touchable one, the incarnation is completed. The human and divine orders are re-united, re-birthed in the fullness of human consciousness. Creation is found good and matter is found holy; nature is not corrupt but sacred, not as spirit nor as matter, but as one in a Love that knows no understanding. That is, as the disciples said, too good to be true, but it is true nonetheless by a wonder beyond all reason. In the most ordinary of acts we disclose the material intimacy of a God who is closer to us than our minds or eyes—for when we eat and drink and touch and sacramentally perform the thousand other acts of human concreteness, we become what we already are, the fellow traveler on the road to Emmaus. This is the good news, this is the great gift —the gift of simply being all in All, love in Love, hope in Hope, faith in Faith.

SCENARIO 5—THE PASSION PLAY

The entire scenario requires three hours and is best done in one session.

Process One—The Entrance into Jerusalem

TIME—Five to fifteen minutes, depending on the number of participants and the length of the line they form

SCRIPTURE—Luke 19:29-38 (read by the guide)

29   *As he drew near to Bethpage and Bethany at the place called the Mount of Olives, he sent two of his disciples.*

30   *He said, "Go into the village opposite you, and as you enter it you will find a colt tethered on which no one has ever sat. Untie it and bring it here.*

31   *And if anyone should ask you, 'Why are you untying it' you will answer, 'The Master has need of it.'"*

32   *So those who had been sent went off and found everything just as he had told them.*

33   *And as they were untying the colt, its owners said to them, "Why are you untying this colt?"*

34   *They answered, "The Master has need of it."*

35   *So they brought it to Jesus, threw their cloaks over the colt, and helped Jesus to mount.*

36   *As he rode along, the people were spreading their cloaks on the road;*

37   *and now as he was approaching the slope of the Mount of Olives, the whole multitude of his disciples began to praise God aloud with joy for all the mighty deeds they had seen.*

38   *They proclaimed: "Blessed is the king who comes in the name of the Lord. Peace in heaven and glory in the highest."*

The reader or guide will say:

Another text uses the word "Hosanna, Hosanna, Hosanna," which roughly translates as "Praise! Praise! Praise!"

Now each of you choose a partner. Stand across

from your partners forming a double line, thus creating a tunnel or arch. This arch is the triumphal line of the entry into Jerusalem.

Now in triumph, move joyfully and rapidly through the arch or tunnel. Begin to sing over and over again, "Hosanna, Heysanna, Sanna, Sanna, Hosanna, Heysanna, Hosanna," from *Jesus Christ, Superstar,* or just sing "Hosanna" and make up your own melody. Now the first pair of partners go through the arch fairly rapidly and very triumphantly. Those who form the arch look at and honor this couple in all their fullness. Having traveled through the entire arch, this pair rejoins the arch at the end. The next couple proceeds down the arch, is honored and rejoins it at the end. So a new arch is being created for other partners to travel through in triumph. Entering your own Jerusalem, come into the fullness of your consummation, feeling its fullness. Continue to sing, "Hosanna, Heysanna, Sanna, Sanna, Hosanna, Heysanna, Hosanna."

Process Two—The Cleansing of the Temple

TIME—Five minutes

SCRIPTURE—Luke 19:45-46 (read by the guide)

45   *Then Jesus entered the temple area and proceeded to drive out those who were selling things,*

46   *saying to them, "It is written, 'My house shall be a house of prayer,' but you have made it a den of thieves."*

The guide says:

After his triumphant entry into Jerusalem, Jesus

went into the Temple and went on a rampage. He threw over the tables of the money lenders, yelling and screaming with a tremendous energy and in full voice, casting out what had sullied the Temple.

For the next few minutes, each of us will move around the room, casting out what has sullied the Temple, the Holy of Holies. Clear out the Temple, the Temple of the planet, the Temple of the school system, the Temple of your life—whatever really makes you mad, that should not be happening. In full voice and rage, cut loose. Name it. Yell it. Stomp around. Cast it out. Begin now. (Five minutes)

(Should voices weaken or spirits flag, the guide will urge the participants on to greater and louder efforts in cleansing the temple.)

Process Three—The Preaching

TIME—Five minutes

SCRIPTURE—Luke 19:47-48; 20:17-26; 21:1-4; 10-12; 25-26; 29-31; 34-36 (read by the guide)

> *19:47   And every day he was teaching in the temple area. The chief priests, the scribes, and the leaders of the people, meanwhile, were seeking to put him to death,*
>
> *48   but they could find no way to accomplish their purpose because all the people were hanging on his words.*
>
> *20:17   But he looked at them and asked, "What then does this scripture passage mean: 'The stone which the builders rejected has become the cornerstone'?*
>
> *18   Everyone who falls on that stone will be dashed to pieces; and it will crush anyone on whom it falls."*

19   The scribes and chief priests sought to lay their hands on him at that very hour, but they feared the people, for they knew that he had addressed this parable to them.

20   They watched him closely and sent agents pretending to be righteous who were to trap him in speech, in order to hand him over to the authority and power of the governor.

21   They posed this question to him, "Teacher, we know that what you say and teach is correct, and you show no partiality, but teach the way of God in accordance with the truth.

22   Is it lawful for us to pay tribute to Caesar, or not?"

23   Recognizing their craftiness he said to them,

24   "Show me a denarius; whose image and name does it bear?" They replied, "Caesar's."

25   So he said to them, "Then repay to Caesar what belongs to Caesar and to God what belongs to God."

26   They were unable to trap him by something he might say before the people, and so amazed were they at his reply that they fell silent.

21:1   When he looked up he saw some wealthy people putting their offerings into the treasury

2   and he noticed a poor widow putting in two small coins.

3   He said, "I tell you truly, this poor widow put in more than all the rest;

4   for those others have all made offerings from their surplus wealth, but she, from her poverty, has offered her whole livelihood."

10   *Then said he to them, "Nation will rise against nation, and kingdom against kingdom.*

11   *There will be powerful earthquakes, famines, and plagues from place to place; and awesome sights and mighty signs will come from the sky.*

12   *Before all this happens, however, they will seize and persecute you, they will hand you over to the synagogues and to prisons, and they will have you led before kings and governors because of my name.*

25   *There will be signs in the sun, the moon, and the stars, and on earth nations will be in dismay, perplexed by the roaring of the sea and the waves.*

26   *People will die of fright in anticipation of what is coming upon the world, for the powers of the heavens will be shaken."*

29   *He taught them a lesson. "Consider the fig tree and all the other trees.*

30   *When their buds burst open, you see for yourselves and know that summer is now near;*

31   *in the same way, when you see these things happening, know that the kingdom of God is near."*

34   *"Beware that your hearts do not become drowsy from carousing and drunkenness and the anxieties of daily life, and that day catch you by surprise*

35   *like a trap. For that day will assault everyone who lives on the face of the earth.*

36   *Be vigilant at all times and pray that you have the strength to escape the tribulations that are imminent and to stand before the Son of Man."*

The guide continues:

Every day Jesus taught in the Temple. He was teaching and teaching and teaching—telling parables and giving answers to crafty questions and warning of the Apocalypse.

This is the time of the great teaching of your heart. Now begin to walk around and preach whatever you have to say, regardless of how inconvenient it is. Speak all those things that you really never dared to say but are in your heart. With your full energy speak the full truth of what you know. Speak the full truth, letting the consequences fall as they will. You are not going to be nice about anything or anybody. You are going to preach your full truth. Begin now. (Five minutes)

Process Four—The Last Supper

TIME—Thirty to forty-five minutes

MATERIALS NEEDED—Enough loaves of bread and a quantity of wine (and/or grape juice) sufficient for the entire group.

SCRIPTURE—Mark 14:1-26 (read by the guide)

1   The Passover and the Feast of Unleavened Bread were to take place in two days' time. So the chief priests and the scribes were seeking a way to arrest him by treachery and put him to death.

2   They said, "Not during the festival, for fear that there may be a riot among the people."

3   When he was in Bethany reclining at table in the house of Simon the leper, a woman came with an ala-

baster jar of perfumed oil, costly genuine spikenard. She broke the alabaster jar and poured it on his head.

4   There were some who were indignant. "Why has there been this waste of perfumed oil?

5   It could have been sold for more than three hundred days' wages and the money given to the poor." They were infuriated with her.

6   Jesus said, "Let her alone. Why do you make trouble for her? She has done a good thing for me.

7   The poor you will always have with you, and whenever you wish you can do good to them, but you will not always have me.

8   She has done what she could. She has anticipated anointing my body for burial.

9   Amen, I say to you, wherever the gospel is proclaimed to the whole world, what she has done will be told in memory of her."

10   Then Judas Iscariot, one of the Twelve, went off to the chief priests, to hand him over to them.

11   When they heard him they were pleased and promised to pay him money. Then he looked for an opportunity to hand him over.

12   On the first day of the Feast of Unleavened Bread, when they sacrificed the Passover lamb, his disciples said to him, "Where do you want us to go and prepare for you to eat the Passover?"

13   He sent two of his disciples and said to them, "Go into the city and a man will meet you, carrying a jar of water. Follow him.

14   Wherever he enters, say to the master of the house,

'The Teacher says, Where is my guest room where I may eat the Passover with my disciples?

15 Then he will show you a large upper room furnished and ready. Make the preparations for us there."

16 The disciples went off, entered the city, and found it just as he had told them; and they prepared the Passover.

17 When it was evening, he came with the Twelve.

18 And as they reclined at table and were eating, Jesus said, "Amen, I say to you, one of you will betray me, one who is eating with me."

19 They began to be distressed and to say to him, one by one, "Surely it is not I?"

20 He said to them, "One of the Twelve, the one who dips with me into the dish.

21 For the Son of man indeed goes, as it is written of him, but woe to that man by whom the Son of man is betrayed! It would be better for that man if he had never been born."

22 While they were eating, he took bread, said the blessing, broke it, and gave it to them, and said, "Take it; this is my body."

23 Then he took the cup, gave thanks, and gave it to them, and they all drank from it.

24 He said to them, "This is my blood of the covenant, which will be shed for many.

25 Amen, I say to you, I shall not drink again the fruit of the vine until the day when I drink it new in the kingdom of God."

26 Then, after singing a hymn, they went out to the Mount of Olives.

The guide continues:

Gather now in groups of three and sit down. Each group will be given a loaf of bread and three glasses of wine (or grape juice).

I ask you now to take a piece of bread and break it, knowing that essentially you are breaking a part of your life, in preparation for the dying of your life. It is the first breaking, and the bread is your body.

And as you do this, we will sing together the old hymn, "Amazing Grace."

Now let the place where you sit in your group become a place of betrayal. Talking among yourselves, tell how you betrayed and how you were the betrayer. Share among the three of you the consequences of that betrayal for your greater vulnerability, for the extension and deepening of your life so that the More could enter in. Betrayal is often a wounding that provides an opening to new life.

As you do this, begin to give the broken pieces of the bread of your life to the others in your group. Eat the bread of each others' lives and drink the wine of their spirits. Eat and drink each others' lives. Begin now. You have about ten minutes.(Ten minutes)

Now, I would like you to see each other betrayers, and forgive each other. Difficult as it may be, give forth the loving. For it is in giving forth and understanding that you are part of a much larger pattern, a much larger story. In giving thanks for the largesse of the story, for the woundings and thus the deepenings of your life, you are no longer hung up on the cross of your life. You are no longer caught in the cave of your dying. Loving brings forth the beginnings of the resurrection of your heart, the extension of the pattern, the honoring of your life.

For the next few minutes, with these others who

have shared the bread and wine and thus have in-
gested the substance of you, see them also as betrayer. In some word or gesture, give them for-
giveness. Give the loving, and thus the releasing. Do
so now. (Five minutes)

Process Five—The Garden of Gethsemane

TIME—Fifteen minutes

SCRIPTURE—Mark 14:32-46 (read by the guide)

32 Then they came to a place named Gethsemane, and he said to his disciples, "Sit here while I pray."

33 He took with him Peter, James, and John, and began to be troubled and distressed.

34 Then he said to them, "My soul is sorrowful even to death. Remain here and keep watch."

35 He advanced a little and fell to the ground and prayed that if it were possible the hour might pass by him;

36 he said, "Abba, Father, all things are possible to you. Take this cup away from me, but not what I will but what you will."

37 When he returned he found them asleep. He said to Peter, "Simon, are you asleep? Could you not keep watch for one hour?

38 Watch and pray that you may not undergo the test. The spirit is willing but the flesh is weak."

39 Withdrawing again, he prayed, saying the same thing.

40   *Then he returned once more and found them asleep,
for they could not keep their eyes open and did not know
what to answer him.*

41   *He returned a third time and said to them, "Are you
still sleeping and taking your rest? It is enough. The
hour has come. Behold, the Son of Man is to be handed
over to sinners.*

42   *Get up, let us go. See, my betrayer is at hand."*

43   *Then, while he was still speaking, Judas, one of the
Twelve, arrived, accompanied by a crowd with swords
and clubs who had come from the chief priests, the
scribes, and the elders.*

44   *His betrayer had arranged a signal with them, saying, "The man I shall kiss is the one; arrest him and lead
him away securely."*

45   *He came and immediately went over to him and
said, "Rabbi." And he kissed him.*

46   *At this they laid hands on him and arrested him.*

The guide continues:

This is the prayer in the Garden, the prayer in
the night. The lights will be dimmed and the room
darkened.

With your eyes closed now, in silence for the next
fifteen minutes of clock time, equal subjectively to a
whole night, review the possibilities of your life. Review the events of your life, its many, many scenes.

In the next minutes review your life in con-
templation or prayer. You can speak with God or the
Beloved of the Soul or whoever in your inner life
shares your most private thoughts. As you review
your life know you have chosen to die. Feel sorrow
for your life soon to end, for the possibilities cut short
and truncated, for the missed opportunities. Do this

as if your life were to end in the next few hours. Take on that whole burden and as you review your life, feel the grief for its ending. (Fifteen minutes)

Process Six—Before Pontius Pilate: "Behold the Man!"

TIME—Approximately fifteen minutes

SCRIPTURE—Luke 23:1-4; 13-16; John 18:37-38; 19:1-5

> *23:1 Then the whole assembly of them arose and brought him before Pilate.*
>
> *2 They brought charges against him, saying, "We found this man misleading our people; he opposes the payment of taxes to Caesar and maintains that he is the Messiah, a king."*
>
> *3 Pilate asked him, "Are you the king of the Jews?" He said to him in reply, "You say so."*
>
> *4 Pilate then addressed the chief priests and the crowds, "I find this man not guilty."*
>
> *13 Pilate then summoned the chief priests, the rulers, and the people*
>
> *14 and said to them, "You brought this man to me and accused him of inciting the people to revolt. I have conducted my investigation in your presence and have not found this man guilty of the charges you have brought against him,*
>
> *15 nor did Herod, for he sent him back to us. So no capital crime has been committed by him.*

16   Therefore I shall have him flogged and then release him."

18:37   So Pilate said to him, "Then you are a king?" Jesus answered, "You say I am a king. For this I was born and for this I came into the world, to testify to the truth. Everyone who belongs to the truth listens to my voice."

38   Pilate said to him, "What is truth?" When he had said this, he again went out to the Jews and said to them, "I find no guilt in him."

19:1   Then Pilate took Jesus and had him scourged.

2   And the soldiers wove a crown out of thorns and placed it on his head, and clothed him in a purple cloak,

3   and they came to him and said, "Hail, King of the Jews!"

4   Once more Pilate went out and said to them, "Look, I am bringing him out to you, so that you may know that I find no guilt in him."

5   So Jesus came out, wearing the crown of thorns and the purple cloak. And he said to them, "Behold the man!"

Ecce Homo! With these words, Jesus was released to be crucified.

Let the lights be turned up again. Now, moving into dyads, play Pilate and Jesus to each other.

The first to be Pilate ask, "Who are you? Who are you really?" In the texts we are told that he was amazed and astonished by Jesus' presence, saying, "There is nothing wrong with this man." He was obviously struck by something. Who are you? Who are you really?

And the one who is the Christos, from the fullness of your being, of your soul, of your presence, with your eyes, without words, answer. Assume the

Christos, knowing yourself as the one who bears the fullness of God, and therefore has to answer nothing. Do this in such a way that even Pilate can say, "Behold the Full Being!"

So let one of you become Pilate and the other Christos, which means the awakened one, the anointed one, the one who is allowing the fullness of your being as Godseed to shine forth. Do this for the next few minutes, and I will tell you when to change. (Five minutes)

And now change roles. Let Christ become Pilate and Pilate become Christ. You who are becoming Christ, let the fullness of the Godseed, of the I AM-ness, rise in you. Let Pilate ask you, "Who are you? Who are you really?" (Five minutes)

Process Seven—Carrying the Cross

TIME—Approximately ten minutes

MUSIC—Philip Glass's "Koyaanisqatsi" is appropriate music for this sequence.

SCRIPTURE—Mark 15:16-22 (read aloud by the guide)

16   The soldiers led him away inside the palace, that is, the praetorium, and assembled the whole cohort.

17   They clothed him in purple and, weaving a crown of thorns, placed it on him.

18   They began to salute him with, "Hail, King of the Jews!"

19   and kept striking his head with a reed and spitting upon him. They knelt before him in homage.

20   And when they had mocked him, they stripped him of the purple cloak, dressed him in his own clothes, and led him out to crucify him.

21   They pressed into service a passer-by, Simon, a Cyrenian, who was coming in from the country, the father of Alexander and Rufus, to carry his cross.

22   They brought him to the place of Golgotha (which is translated Place of the Skull).

The guide continues:

Now I ask you to stand up, remembering who your partner is, because you will eventually come back to this place.

Now as the music plays, begin to take up your life, as if you were carrying a cross. The whole of your life will be your cross. Actually bend as if you were carrying the whole burden of your life. Move around this room with that cross, the burdens of your life which you are about to lay down. That is the fullness of your life—its beauty, its tragedy, its glory and its burden.

Feel the weight of that whole life. The lights will be lowered again, and you will walk in darkness with the weight of your life up to Golgotha, there to be crucified, there to end the life.

Individually, alone, in silence, carry the cross of your life. Know its full burden, beautiful and terrible as your life may have been. Carry the full burden of it.

It may be not only the burden of your life. It may be the burden of life lived today, or the burden of all lives, of all those for whom you have compassion— the needy and hungry, the ones who are born with broken brains and bodies, the ones born into lives with no opportunities, so that they will never have a chance. Carry the burden of their lives as well. (Five to ten minutes)

Process Eight—The Crucifixion

TIME—Five minutes

SCRIPTURE—Mark 15:24-37 (read by the guide)

24   Then they crucified him and divided his garments by casting lots for them to see what each should take.

25   It was nine o'clock in the morning when they crucified him.

26   The inscription of the charge against him read, "The King of the Jews."

27   With him they crucified two revolutionaries, one on his right and one on his left.

28   And the scripture was fulfilled that says, "And he was counted among the wicked."

29   Those passing by reviled him, shaking their heads and saying, "Aha! You who would destroy the temple and rebuild it in three days,

30   save yourself by coming down from the cross."

31   Likewise the chief priests, with the scribes, mocked him among themselves and said, "He saved others; he cannot save himself.

32   Let the Messiah, the King of Israel, come down now from the cross that we may see and believe." Those who were crucified with him also kept abusing him.

33   At noon darkness came over the whole land until three in the afternoon.

34   And at three o'clock Jesus cried out in a loud voice, "Eloi, Eloi, lama sabachthani?" which is translated, "My God, my God, why have you forsaken me?"

35   Some of the bystanders who heard it said, "Look, he is calling Elijah."

36   One of them ran, soaked a sponge with wine, put it on a reed, and gave it to him to drink, saying, "Wait, let us see if Elijah comes to take him down."

37   Jesus gave a loud cry and breathed his last.

The guide continues:

Now we will take on a very difficult process. We will perform our own crucifixion. We're going to perform the Cross of Gold.

Now find the partner with whom you played the roles of Pilate and Jesus. This process lasts only four or five minutes, but it is very difficult. During it you will probably feel "My God, My God, why hast thou forsaken me?" You may feel the conscious crucifixion of your own body and life.

Facing your partner, stand with your arms raised to each side at shoulder height, so that your body forms a cross. That's all, but it will last for five minutes.

After a few minutes you are going to feel a lot of pain. When you think you can't stand it any longer, you will stand it longer. And when you think you cannot stand it any longer than that, you will stand it still longer. When you feel that you absolutely cannot stand it longer, then stand it longer, that the Spirit may fill you, that you may begin to break down the old resistances, the old habits that make you cling to deadening life.

Begin to watch what you call fatigue or pain. Just watch, for in that you will also discover what liberates. Stay with it so that you begin to discover what liberates you from your crucifixion.

As you do this, face your partner, who in a few

minutes will also probably be in a lot of pain. You will encourage and sustain each other and give each other the strength to "hang in there."

If you must groan like Jesus, then groan. You are not running away from pain at this point. You groan not just for yourself, but for all Creation, for the pain that you feel is but a small portion of the agony that pervades Creation at this time.

Then at a certain point—actually a very few minutes, though it may seem to you a hundred hours on the cross, or a hundred years—I will tell you to release and just let go.

Now, facing your partner, raise your arms and begin the Cross of Gold.

(During the period of this exercise, the Guide will offer encouragement to the participants.)

Just groan, and keep your arms up. You are groaning for all Creation—for the hungry and for the bereft, for the land being ravaged—the pain of the whole earth.

Groan for your life, groan for what you are about to release, groan for all of Creation.

Even if the pain is too great, hang in there and keep your arms up, encouraging your partner to do so with you.

Stay with it. Keep your arms up. Watch your strength. Watch what liberates you.

Let the groans out; groan for Creation. (Five minutes)

Process Nine—Death and the Tomb/Womb

TIME—Approximately twelve minutes

MUSIC—Hovhannes, *The Mysterious Mountain* or Fauré *Requiem.*

The guide continues:

Release, let go, fall off the cross, and die. Release and fall to the ground. Come to quiet.

This is the beginning of the great Middle Eastern mystery of initiation, the reconstitution in the tomb that takes three days. This is the beginning of the giving up of your life so that you can take on the extended life of greater complexity and larger patterns. You are no longer weeping for your life. This is the time in which you have agreed to your own dying. You have looked at yourself as betrayer and betrayed. You have known the fullness of your being. You have known something of the fullness of human suffering. You have carried the cross of your life and have suffered upon it. You have groaned for all Creation. And now, as of this moment, you have entered the tomb/womb of your own regeneration where you take on the fetus of Higher Being.

We are told in the mystery tradition that the Christos who resides in you, joined now in the ancient gnostic tradition to the Sophia, becomes the Beloved of the Soul. We are told that Jesus descended unto Hell, and there he forgave all people for their unskilled behavior. He forgave the desperate, the homicidal, the smug. He forgave the rapists, the ones who sowed dissension in the hearts of others and the ones whose lives had been destructive. He forgave. In some sense you will descend now into the hell of your own being, and there you will forgive the hellish ones there and your own hellish acts. (Three minutes)

We are told that he ascended into Heaven to the Extended Kingdom, where he joined in partnership with the Extended Reality, with the realm of forms and creativity of the godded world. He entered into the partnership of Love. Now you enter into the deep and extended heaven of your own being, and there agree to take on partnership with the Extended Reality, partnership with God. (Three minutes)

There was a long time of silence as Jesus' psyche-mind-body was rewoven, restructured and made available to pulse in a new rhythm of consciousness. Feel yourself in the Womb of Higher Being. Feel yourself rewoven, pulsed, extended in your nerves and sinews, in your brain and body, in your heart and soul, in your deep mind. The new fetus, the new child, the new being is now growing in you. Enter this place of restructuring, of reweaving, of resonating to a deeper pulse, so that when you come back you can be a pulse of new possibility for those around you. (Three minutes)

You will now hear a song with roots so ancient that it could have been heard by Jesus in his time. As the music plays, feel yourself to be the new fetus, the new child, the new one now being rewoven.

Process Ten—The Resurrection

TIME—Approximately twenty to thirty minutes

SCRIPTURE—Luke 24:1-11 (read by the guide)

24:1   But at daybreak on the first day of the week they took the spices they had prepared and went to the tomb.

2   They found the stone rolled away from the tomb;

3   but when they entered, they did not find the body of the Lord Jesus.

4   *While they were puzzling over this, behold, two men in dazzling garments appeared to them.*

5   *They were terrified and bowed their faces to the ground. They said to them, "Why do you seek the living one among the dead?*

6   *He is not here, but he has been raised. Remember what he said to you while he was still in Galilee,*

7   *that the Son of Man must be handed over to sinners and be crucified, and rise on the third day."*

8   *And they remembered his words.*

9   *Then they returned from the tomb and announced all these things to the eleven and to all the others.*

10   *The women were Mary Magdalene, Joanna, and Mary the mother of James; the others who accompanied them also told this to the apostles,*

11   *but their story seemed like nonsense and they did not believe them.*

The guide continues:

And now begin to draw breath up, not just breath but prana, extended breath, vital energy. Draw it up through the soles of your feet. Feel it coming up the legs into the knees, along the spine, and then out through the very center of the top of the head. New connections are being made in this new being. Like a fetus, begin to be constituted. Feel the roots, the way you are held by Mother Earth. Feel the livingness, the vitality, the generosity of this earth you are lying on. Allow your spine and your feet simply to appreciate being cradled in the Womb of Becoming, being held, being given an anchor in the placenta of this universe.

You are listening now with your spine, and

voices that you do not often hear are speaking to you. You are feeling vibrations, music, rhythms that come to the very core of the planet from outside, through cosmic space. Feel this cosmic pulsation like mighty quasars loaded with the music of the times. It comes quaking through you, implanting the higher genetic code, a higher being.

Breathing, grounding, being nourished by the blood of the Mother, by the energies of Creation, take in the vitalizing breath of existence, energy for each cell. Breathe not just oxygen, but the vital creative force made up of the magical transubstantiation of water and plants and minerals as they live in sunlight. The rays of the star, the holy star, mix with the green of the earth, so as you breathe you breathe the Beloveds, the sun and the earth. The Sun representing the Logos, the great organizing principle of Creation, is now being breathed through you. The great Logos is being taken up in transubstantiation into all your cells, each one. The deeper life principle is now moving through you.

Just as your breathing in nourishes you with this mysterious combination of life and star, your breathing out nourishes the plants and the planet. With every breath you breathe in your connection to the cosmos, for you are a very large fetus connected by the navel cord to the solar system. With every sensation you imbibe the vibrations of cosmic space that go into your resurrection, into your re-creation. You do not need to go anywhere to find the parents that nourish you. Christos and Sophia, the Awakened One and Wisdom herself are recreating you now. You need only to be—without doing. Listen and feel with your body. This is the fetal loom for the Beloved. This is the grounding for the expression of the Love which cradles you and nourishes you with every breath.

Now is the key moment of resurrection. Place your hands over the center of your chest, either on your physical body or not quite on the physical body. At that place let your hands explore the love, the energy, that is coming out of the cave, the cave of the chest. That cave is where you as an initiate lie dormant; it is the door to your resurrection. The heart cavity is opening, allowing you to flow into all and everything. Feel that flow with your hands.

Let your hands speak to your chest, to the center of the chest, the high chest. Touch that energy, for you are touching the Holy Beloved. Know that in this human body, that place in the chest is the place of receiving and being. It is the cave of the long sleep, and you may have been asleep for many, many years. It is the cave of awakening, the resurrection from a life that has failed to really be, that has failed to perceive what is around it, that has failed to live itself— the life that is now crucified and over.

The Beloved of the Soul is lying there inside, waiting only for the contact of your hands. That which fashioned the universe, from the tiniest ants to the farthest star—that which creates the seasons and all of life, that which creates the mysteries of the black holes, of the great nebulae, that which creates the coded genius that is there in the egg of a flea—all this lies within the cave, this tomb. It is loving you and yearning for communion with you if only you will love it, if only you will bother to make the contact and risk opening and realizing that you are deeply loved.

Let your hands begin to feel and appreciate what comes from inside. Let your chest appreciate the energy that comes from the hand. Lift your hand off the body a bit in a dialogue between the Beloved and the lover, between the evocateur lover which is the hand and the inside lover who sometimes seems to close the door to the cave but is always waiting, yearning to be reunited. The hand and the heart can speak to each other in the wordless language of love.

Begin to make a sound that comes from within you. Sing to this lover within, crooning just slightly, telling this Beloved that you know that you are loving union for life, and that life is eternity. Hmmmm—Hmmmm—Hmmmm. You and your Beloved cannot be separated; you can only forget to make the contact. Hear the lovers sing to each other. You hear that everything around you is singing, that you are lying in your Mother's arms, that the breath of life is streaming into you. Each cell and tissue and molecule and system and organ of you is reconstituting Sophia and Christos together, reweaving a new life. The Beloved is now giving you the psychic depth, the empathy, the energy, the desire to be and to live as fully as you can and as you are.

Beginning now, slowly move, open your eyes and sit up. This is the resurrection. We move, we sit, we walk upon the earth. This is my Body. Cradled, we walk and sit upon the Earth. We are not separated from our Beloved. And so rise as the lights begin to come on. Know that within you the Body of Resurrection is there now, reconstituted. Feel yourself in communion with your Beloved, so that you will not be separated from anyone or anything ever again. Slowly come to dance with the Lord of the Dance. Roll away the stone now—here you have help—and see others as God no longer in hiding.

Dance, then, wherever you may be,
I am the Lord of the Dance, said he,
And I'll lead you all, wherever you may be,
And I'll lead you all in the dance, said he.

I danced in the morning when the world was
    begun,
And I danced in the moon and the stars and the
    sun,
And I came down from heaven and I danced on the
    earth—
At Bethlehem I had my birth.

I danced for the scribe and the Pharisee,
But they would not dance and they wouldn't
    follow me;
I danced for the fishermen, for James and John—
They came with me and the dance went on.

I danced on the Sabbath and I cured the lame;
The holy people said it was a shame;
They whipped and they stripped and they hung
    me high,
And they left me there on a cross to die.

I danced on a Friday and the sky turned black.
It's hard to dance with the devil on your back;
They buried my body and they thought I'd gone.
But I am the dance and I still go on.

They cut me down and I leap up high—
I am the life that'll never, never die;
I'll live in you if you'll live in me—
I am the Lord of the Dance, said he.

Dance, then, wherever you may be,
I am the Lord of the Dance, said he,
And I'll lead you all, wherever you may be,
And I'll lead you all in the dance, said he.

(Based on a Shaker tune, "'Tis a gift to be simple . . . ." Words written, and music arranged and
adapted by Sydney Carter, 1963.)

Process Eleven—The Road to Emmaus

TIME—The rest of your life

SCRIPTURE—Luke 24: 13-21; 28-43; 49-53

24:13   Now that very day two of them were going to a village seven miles from Jerusalem called Emmaus,

14   and they were conversing about all the things that had occurred.

15   And it happened that while they were conversing and debating, Jesus himself drew near and walked with them,

16   but their eyes were prevented from recognizing him.

17   He asked them, "What are you discussing as you walk along?" They stopped, looking downcast.

18   One of them, named Cleopas, said to him in reply, "Are you the only visitor to Jerusalem who does not know of the things that have taken place there in these days?"

19   And he replied to them, "What sort of things?" They said to him, "The things that happened to Jesus the Nazarene, who was a prophet mighty in deed and word before God and all the people,

20   how our chief priests and rulers both handed him over to a sentence of death and crucified him.

21   But we were hoping that he would be the one to redeem Israel; and besides all this, it is now the third day since this took place."

28   As they approached the village to which they were going, he gave the impression that he was going on farther.

29   But they urged him, "Stay with us, for it is nearly evening and the day is almost over." So he went in to stay with them.

30   And it happened that, while he was with them at table, he took bread, said the blessing, broke it, and gave it to them.

31   With that their eyes were opened and they recognized him, but he vanished from their sight.

32   Then they said to each other, "Were not our hearts burning (within us) while he spoke to us on the way and opened the scriptures to us?"

33   So they set out at once and returned to Jerusalem where they found gathered together the eleven and those with them

34   who were saying, "The Lord has truly been raised and has appeared to Simon!"

35   Then the two recounted what had taken place on the way and how he was made known to them in the breaking of the bread.

36   While they were still speaking about this, he stood in their midst and said to them, "Peace be with you."

37   But they were startled and terrified and thought that they were seeing a ghost.

38   Then he said to them, "Why are you troubled? And why do questions arise in your hearts?

39   Look at my hands and my feet, that it is I myself. Touch me and see, because a ghost does not have flesh and bones as you can see I have."

40   And as he said this, he showed them his hands and his feet.

41   While they were still incredulous for joy and were

amazed, he asked them, "Have you anything here to eat?"

42   *They gave him a piece of baked fish;*

43   *he took it and ate it in front of them.*

49   *"And behold I am sending the promise of my Father upon you; but stay in the city until you are clothed with power from on high."*

50   *Then he led them out as far as Bethany, raised his hands, and blessed them.*

51   *As he blessed them he parted from them and was taken up to heaven.*

52   *They did him homage and then returned to Jerusalem with great joy,*

53   *and they were continually in the temple praising God.*

The Road to Emmaus is the road to the rest of your life. When you leave this room you will be on that road as the Godseed, your divine essence fully incorporated in your human form and your human form delighting in sharing the pleasures of human companionship. Go forth now, as Godseeds, in the full knowledge of your resurrection to a new way of being. Go forth with a willingness to live in an extended body, an amplified mind, a compassionate heart, a deepened soul, and a new life of high service to whomever and whatever comes your way. Be a friend on the road of life to all whom you meet, always servant and never lord. Listen deeply to their stories as they tell of the passion play of their life, and wherever warranted, give counsel from that part of you that is the living Christic force that can never die. Above all, see the God-in-Hiding everywhere and in everyone. And never cease to be astonished.

Music Selections

The following selections are recommended for the various processes in the Godseed journey. The reader should regard them as only suggestions and should feel free to use his or her own favorites, trying to keep them within the mood and intention of the process described.

Samuel Barber: Adagio for Strings. RCA AGLI-3790
Ferde Grofé, The Grand Canyon Suite. Various recordings
Chaltanya Hari Deuter, Ecstacy. KucKuck 044
Philip Glass, Koyaanisqatsi. Antilles-Island ZCASTA-1
Gregorian Chants. Various recordings
Alan Hovhaness, Mysterious Mountain. RCA AGLI-4215
Georgia Kelly, Seapeace. Heru Records
Marin Marais, La Sonnerie, in Perles du Baroque, Cassette ARN 436342
Pachelbel: Canon in D. Musical Heritage 1060Z
Tomita, Kosmos. RCA ARL 1-2616
Tomita, Snowflakes Are Dancing. RCA ARL 10488

All of the recordings listed above as well as other suitable recordings are available from:

Mickey Houlihan
Wind Over the Earth
1688 Redwood Avenue
Boulder, CO 80504
Phone: 800 726-0847

Picture Credits

QUEST BOOKS
are published by
The Theosophical Society in America,
Wheaton, Illinois 60189-0270,
a branch of a world organization
dedicated to the promotion of brotherhood and
the encouragement of the study of religion,
philosophy, and science, to the end that man may
better understand himself and his place in
the universe. The Society stands for complete
freedom of individual search and belief.
In the Classics Series well-known
theosophical works are made
available in popular editions.

Q
QUEST
BOOKS

We publish books on:
Health and Healing
Mysticism • Transpersonal Psychology
Philosophy • Religion • Reincarnation
Theosophical Philosophy • Yoga and Meditation

Other books of possible interest include:

Acknowledge the Wonder *by Frances Wosmek*
Inspires a renewed sense of wonder and oneness with nature.

Fullness of Human Experience *by Dane Rudhyar*
How cyclic nature of creation affects our psychic evolution.

Glorious Presence *by Ernest Wood*
The Vendanta philosophy.

Gnostic Jung & Seven Sermons to the Dead *by Stephan Hoeller*
Based on a little-known treatise Jung authored.

Jungian Symbolism in Astrology *by Alice O. Howell*
Birthcharts and psychotherapy are integrated.

The Radiant Child *by Thomas Armstrong*
Mystical and transpersonal experiences in children.

Rhythm of Wholeness *by Dane Rudhyar*
The world as an interdependent evolutionary process.

Walk On! *by Christmas Humphreys*
An inspirational book on the art of living.

When the Sun Moves Northward *by Mabel Collins*
Spiritual regeneration and the earth's seasonal rebirth.

Available from:
The Theosophical Publishing House
P.O. Box 270, Wheaton, IL 60189-0270

NOTES

NOTES